MW00874344

FAITHFULLY FAITHFUL

Devotionals

CRYSTAL FRY

Faithfully Faithful
Copyright © 2019 Crystal Fry

All rights reserved. No portion of this book may be reproduced, stored in a retrieval system, or transmitted in any form or by any means electronic, mechanical, photocopy, recording, scanning, or other, without prior written permission of the publisher.

All Scripture quotations, unless otherwise indicated, are taken from the The ESV Bible The Holy Bible, English Standard Version, copyright © 2001 by Crossway, a publishing ministry of Good News Publishers. Used by permission. All rights reserved.

Scripture noted from The Message. Copyright © 1993, 1994, 1995, 1996, 2000, 2001, 2002. Used by permission of NavPress Publishing Group.

Scripture quotations marked (NIV) are taken from the Holy Bible, New International Version®, NIV®. Copyright © 1973, 1978, 1984, 2011 by Biblica, Inc.™ Used by permission of Zondervan. All rights reserved worldwide. www.zondervan.com The "NIV" and "New International Version" are trademarks registered in the United States Patent and Trademark Office by Biblica, Inc.™

Scripture quotations marked (NLT) are taken from the Holy Bible, New Living Translation, copyright ©1996, 2004, 2015 by Tyndale House Foundation. Used by permission of Tyndale House Publishers, Inc., Carol Stream, Illinois 60188. All rights reserved.

All rights reserved.

DEDICATION

I dedicate **Faithfully Faithful** to two beautiful ladies:

Virginia Flinn, my sweet mama. I am so thankful for all the
years and time you spent pouring the love of God into me.
You have never given up on me and spent countless hours I
know praying over me. I believe your faithfulness to
pouring seeds into me is one of the many reasons this book
is coming to fruition. My love for daily time with God first
started at your table each morning where I was able to hear
and read your devotions at breakfast with you. I love you to
the moon and back forever and ever. I will forever be
grateful that God made you my grandmother.

Aunt Betty, your passion for life was contagious. Your
smile and laughter could light up a room. This is for you.
You had a dream of being an author, and I'm sure you are
writing many novels now in heaven.

ACKNOWLEDGEMENTS

To those this wouldn't have happened without,

My sweet husband, you never stop encouraging me to live out all my dreams. Thank you for always standing behind me every step of the way.

Heather and Kenny Sides, this wouldn't be happening without your dedication to making the first handmade copy. Heather, you poured so much love into helping me get all of these pages together. You both are a blessing to my family, and I thank you for pushing me the extra mile. My heart will forever be grateful for the countless hours you two spent. Thank you seems so small.

My soul sister, Ashley, thank you for always encouraging me beyond my limits and never letting me give up on my goals.

My coworker, Shannon, thank you for motivating me to start an email account for my daily devotions.

Allison Cain, thank you for mentoring me through this process and believing in me.

All my other family and friends, thank you for instilling a sense of God's love in me along the way. Thank you all for cheering me on, motivating me, and believing in my dream as much as I did.

To my book cover designer,

Katie Carroll, thank you for taking a vision I had from the beginning and creating something better than I could have imagined with your talent. I am so incredibly thankful for you.

To my book editor,

Amy Sessoms, thank you for spending countless hours doing something that takes a ton of patience. I am forever grateful that you shared your time and energy on this book for me.

To everyone reading this,

I pray that in some way my love for God is projected through these pages onto you and that through reading these devotions you feel closer, stronger, and more planted in His grace than ever before. I hope every day you find His love in these scriptures and words. I am blessed by you giving me the chance to love on you by reflecting the love that He has shined on me. I am truly humbled.

INTRODUCTION

What is Faithfully Faithful? Sometimes God makes you uncomfortable so that you can seek His comfort in your life. This is what He did with me early one morning as I sat spending my quiet time with Him.

For months I had written devotions in a journal from scriptures I would read during our one-on-one time. One morning He laid it on my heart to share them. I fought back and forth with Him saying all sorts of things, such as, "These people are going to think I am crazy. Why would they even want to read this? Lord, this is just me journaling my expressions and they aren't meant to be shared." Finally, after feeling that push more and more, I started sending them to the ladies in my life group. Their support, constant love, and encouragement shined a light into why God pushed me out of my comfort zone to share the things He had laid on my heart. As I began to read through a book on purpose, I began to realize that this is what God was working on inside of me. A purpose to serve Him with a talent that He blessed me with, words. These devotions became my heart for Him expressed with pen and paper. Soon after I began to write these devotions, He not only led me to connecting with people through art, He also led me to a friendship that I so desperately needed and a ministry of ladies that I would have the pleasure to love on. He is such a good Father.

The life I sometimes chose to live and the life that was dealt for me wasn't always the shiniest. It wasn't glitter and gold, but God sure paved a path for me that shined brighter than any diamond. For a long time, I looked at my life from a "why me" standpoint until one day I realized I wanted God to use me - all the ugly, dirty, and broken pieces of me. That's when I realized He was making beauty out of ashes. My testimony is for another time, but my God has always been so faithful to me. I knew it was time for me to be faithfully faithful to Him. This is my heart.

Week One

Day 1

MIND ON THE BLESSING

Blessings are sure to come, although sometimes they may just seem far away. It's not because of anything God has done, but sometimes we can lose sight of what we wanted Him to bless us with in the first place.

Put your mind on the blessing. When we focus on God and remain faithful to Him, He can produce our full potential. We can bear our fruit.

But blessed is the one who trusts in the Lord, whose confidence is in him. They will be like a tree planted by the water that sends out its roots by the stream. It does not fear when heat comes; its leaves are always green. It has no worries in a year of drought and never fails to bear fruit. Jeremiah 17:7-8 (NIV)

Blessed are those who face opposition and do not fear because they know God is near. Those who have their roots planted deep within the Lord can withstand whatever may come their way. They water their faith daily which allows their roots to be planted firmly within the word. When our roots are planted within the one who matters, we can see blessings even when the blessing has not yet come.

Keeping your mind on the blessing is having a faith bigger than the storm.

Day 2

WHO IS ON YOUR WALK?

God doesn't want us to be alone in the world. If He did, he wouldn't have created a companion for Adam, and He wouldn't have allowed the world to multiply. God wants us to have companionship. He wants us to have company, others to do life with. He created us all with purpose to spread His name and to live out our calling. He gives us friendships to help us along the way. As we choose our path, we also choose our friends.

Two are better than one, because they have good return for their labor: If either of them falls down, one can help the other up. But pity anyone who falls and has no one to help them up. Ecclesiastes 4:9-10 (NIV)

As iron sharpens iron, so one person sharpens another. Proverbs 27:17 (NIV)

Friendship is powerful. The Bible says a lot about choosing friends wisely and being good counsel for your friends. We could find multiple verses that tell us to wisely choose with whom we associate. When we are led by the wrong counsel, we can begin to be blinded in our own walk. However, when we have others who sharpen us, we have a blessing from God. I'm a firm believer that God sends us others to learn from, to grow with, and to teach. He gives us full reign on whom we allow to enter our lives and walk beside us. Be careful about whom you allow to join you on your walk. Not everyone was meant for you; not everyone was meant to be on your path.

Day 3

HE IS OUR CONTENTMENT

Contentment can be hard for some; it's hard for a lot of people to decipher their needs from their wants. We all tend to want a lot more than we need.

Contentment comes from inside of you. It comes from a place where your satisfaction is no longer based on wants or needs but is based on God. When we are content in the Lord, we truly have everything we can ever need or want.

But godliness with contentment is great gain, for we brought nothing into this world, and we cannot take anything out of the world.
1 Timothy 6:6-7

God wants our hearts to be content in all parts of our lives. He wants no love to come before Him, and He desires that we fully trust in Him for all our needs in this life.

Let's try to be more content in our walk with the Lord, knowing He is our place of happiness and satisfaction. Nothing can compare to the contentment He can bring.

Day 4

HAVE IT MEMORIZED

I don't always have to see God's goodness in my life to believe it is there because I already have it memorized.

We should have God's goodness memorized so well that we don't need to see it to believe it. When we memorize what he has done for us already, we know what He can do for us in the future.

A good way to always remember this is to take a prayer journal and write down your prayers. God's faithfulness will show up time and time again on those pages of prayer.

We choose to remember what we want, and then we let go of the rest. I don't think God wants us to just remember pieces, He wants us to remember it all. He wants us to remember what He's done. When we start to remember what He has done for us, we are memorizing His goodness and faithfulness to us. It's the way we memorize it that matters. We must look at it from the outcome and not from the journey. Writing down prayers makes a huge difference in the way we choose to see what He's doing.

We all need to think of ways we can memorize God's power and glory, so we know how to praise Him even through the opposition.

Let all that I am praise the Lord; may I never forget the good things he does for me. Psalms 103:2 (NLT)

Day 5

CALL ON HIM

Relax
Take a deep breath...
What's bothering you?
Nothing is bigger than God!

I don't know about you, but sometimes in the midst of trouble, I forget to stop and go to the one that can truly help. It can seem that friends are better able to meet our needs at the time, but friends aren't always going to have the answer. We tend to forget that God wants to hear from us.

Just as we pick up the phone to call a friend, God wants us to pick up the pieces and call on Him.

No one is as prepared as He is. He is the ultimate healer! He restores, comforts, and replenishes. There is no love compared to the love He is equipped to give us in our times of need.

When you concede defeat, you are allowing the enemy to creep in.

In God there is only victory!

I have told you these things, so that in me you may have peace. In this world you will have trouble. But take heart! I have overcome the world. John 16:33 (NIV)

Day 6

HANDWRITTEN

Ever heard that saying, "Don't judge a book by its cover?" You know, our lives are all a story. The outside of us is our cover. The inside might start off with some good chapters, then get to some that no one wants to read, including yourself, but if you quit reading there how in the world would you get to the best part at the end? You know your book; my book doesn't end until He's done writing it. Every chapter is delicately designed, but if we judged every book by its cover, we may never know all the good that lies inside of it.

No one should ever be judged by the exterior of their book especially when the interior of it has been handwritten by God himself. The beauty of your story may be in those chapters that didn't start off that well but ended with great purpose.

Your eyes saw my unformed substance; in your book were written, every one of them, the days that were formed for me, when as yet there was none of them.
Psalm 139:16

God has planned your story so don't allow yourself to sign where it says, "Author." I want the last sentence in my book to say, *"Well done my good and faithful servant."* For I know He truly makes beauty from ashes.

Journal

Day 7

Take time to meditate on God's word. What's on your
heart this week?

_____

_____

_____

_____

_____

_____

_____

_____

_____

_____

_____

_____

_____

_____

_____

_____

_____

_____

Week Two

Day 1

YOU ARE PERSONALIZED

As humans we all tend to focus on our imperfections. I know I have pointed out my own imperfections within the last week, probably even yesterday. I'm learning every day that imperfections aren't flaws but are parts of our character. They provide distinction within us. They build us and help define us.

We sometimes dwell on our imperfections negatively:
• I'm not good enough or this isn't good enough.
• I don't look good or I'd like to look the same as that person.
• I don't like this about myself.
• I want to change this about me, or I want to change this about something I've done.

God knew that perfect people could not be used in an imperfect world. Your imperfections may be just what God needs for another person to see that He uses us all just the way He created us. He doesn't want us to all be the same. Just as He gave us all distinct talents and gifts, He designed us all as imperfect people to help touch an imperfect world.

All of us have been carefully designed with individuality and distinctiveness. When God personalized you, He didn't have me in mind.

We need to remember when we look at ourselves that we shouldn't be wishing or hoping for anything other than what God has created within us. What we see as imperfections, God sees as beauty. If the King of Kings and the Lord of

Lords views us as beautiful, why do we need any other affirmation of who we are? We are just downright beautiful!

You are altogether beautiful, my darling; there is no flaw in you. Song of Songs 4:7 (NIV)

Day 2

WREAK HAVOC

With a new year comes new goals, and at the end of a year we will have accomplished some, taken a step back from others, and completely shoved the rest under a rug to come back to next year. At the beginning of a year, it's a time of reflection to start new beginnings.

I'd like to think of this not just as a new beginning, but a new opportunity to fall deeper in love with our Savior. A time that we can seek Him more by drawing in closer to what He wants for our lives. We can together wreak havoc on the enemy instead of him wreaking havoc on us.

let us go right into the presence of God with sincere hearts fully trusting him. For our guilty consciences have been sprinkled with Christ's blood to make us clean, and our bodies have been washed with pure water.
Hebrews 10:22 (NLT)

Let's break this scripture down some into what He wants from us.

1. What does it mean to have a TRUE heart?
True is a characteristic of God. It also means accurate or exact. Having a true heart would be having your heart based off truth. We can find the truth in the word. Drawing near to God is having a heart full of HIS truths over our lives.

2. What is having a heart FULL OF ASSURANCE of faith?
When we are full of assurance in ourselves, we are confident, but we are only truly confident when we are full

of assurance in our faith. We need to have full confidence in our faith and the One who gave us the gift of salvation. Having a heart full of assurance is having confidence in Christ.

3. How do we sprinkle our hearts clean from an evil conscience?
Drawing closer to God means cleansing the depths of our hearts. Sometimes that may be painful, but truthfully, growing should be painful. We should want God to take anything away from us that is not of Him and purify the depths of our souls to be more like Him. He has to clean us from the inside out.

4. Now let us wash our bodies with pure water.
We have to wash ourselves in truth, in his full assurance, cleaning out all evil. We do this by reading His scripture, knowing who He is, and making a platform that is our rock to stand on in the way we live our lives.

This year I pray that we all draw our hearts closer to God, that we take steps to grow our faith, and that we live in the confident assurance of His truth!

Day 3

PUT YOUR TRUST IN HIM

God was calling Jonah to go to Ninevah to preach because He saw what the city was doing and how their hearts were in the wrong place. Jonah didn't want to listen to what God was calling him to do; instead, Jonah decided to get on a ship to Tarshish.

Jonah wanted to flee from God much like we do when we don't want to do something God is calling us to do.

When Jonah got on the boat, the seas started to roar, and the men knew that someone had caused this. Jonah confessed that God had called him, but he had gone astray.

Even though Jonah was not where God wanted Him, this is a perfect example of how God still uses us where we are. The men on the boat were able to see how God's word is true. Jonah was still reaching others with God's word by being a testimony for where he was and how important it is to follow when God is calling you.

Jonah was thrown into the sea and spent three days and three nights inside a fish. There Jonah prayed.

"I called out to the Lord, out of my distress, and he answered me; out of the belly of Sheol I cried, and you heard my voice." Jonah 2:2

God hears us no matter where we are! We can be in the darkest of places, but when we call on God, He is always near. He fights each fight with us hand in hand.

Jonah continued to pray.

"I went down to the land whose bars closed upon me forever; yet you brought up my life from the pit, O Lord my God." Jonah 2:6

God is merciful. We serve a forgiving God. He did not promise that there would not be battles when we stray, but He did promise that no matter where we are, He would be right beside us.

Put your trust in God today and follow where He is calling.

Day 4

STAND UP

God's plan for your life is far greater than anything you can compose.

Being an example as a Christ-follower is probably one of the hardest things to do, especially in a world where many times evil is paid back with evil. As Christians, we have an obligation not to please ourselves but to put others before us.

We who are strong have an obligation to bear with the failings of the weak, and not to please ourselves.
Romans 15:1

God wants us to share humility through our faith. He wants us to stand down from what almost feels "normal" in today's world and to stand up for what we know is right. The weak need the strong just as the strong sometimes have lessons to learn from the weak.

God gave us each other to lift and to help, to build up and not to tear down.

We all have something to give and to share.

Therefore welcome one another as Christ has welcomed you, for the glory of God. Romans 15:7

Extend open arms!

Day 5

THEY DON'T DEFINE YOU

Blessed be the God and Father of our Lord Jesus Christ, the Father of mercies and God of all comfort, who comforts us in all our affliction, so that we may be able to comfort those who are in any affliction, with the comfort with which we ourselves are comforted by God. For as we share abundantly in Christs sufferings, so through Christ we share abundantly in comfort too. 2 Corinthians 1:3-5

Everyone has some sort of scars. It could be physical scars that came from falling off a bike, or it could be an internal scar that may not be so apparent, like something you went through as a child. Either way our scars usually tell some sort of story. We must be careful not to allow our internal scars to become a negative definition of who we are. Our internal scars that aren't so apparent are usually the ones that take the longest to heal. Those scars are the ones that we can either learn to allow God to use to help impact others, or we can choose to let them define us.

Scars usually are looked at as a bad thing. When we are hurt so badly physically or internally that it leaves a scar, we are left with memories that won't leave us. God wants us to use our scars. He doesn't want our scars to hold us back. He wants to heal and restore them. God doesn't want our scars to be used as a crutch; He wants to use them as a testimony. Scars allow us to help others. God can use your scars to be a blessing to someone else. Don't allow your scars to define who you are. You are only defined by God your Father. Allow your scars to be a testimony of what God can and will do if you allow Him to use you to further His kingdom.

Day 6

THE GIFT THAT'S FREE

When someone gives you a gift, what do you do with it? You appreciate it, show thankfulness for it, and use it.

Well, God has given us the best gift of all, and that's the gift of salvation, the gift of eternal life. What are you doing with the gift He's given you?

The biggest gift we could ever receive was given to us when Christ died on the cross for our sins. We tend to push that to the side just as any tangible thing we receive here. When we accept Jesus into our hearts, and we pray the sinner's prayer, the gift that we have been given should be put higher than any gift we could ever receive here on earth.

For the wages of sin is death, but the free gift of God is eternal life in Christ Jesus our Lord. Romans 6:23

How are we treating the most meaningful gift of all? This is something that should cross all of our minds. Are we thankful for it? Do we thank God daily for the gift He gave and continues to give us through His grace and mercy, even when we continue to fail and sin? Do we appreciate the love He shows us daily and the hope he gives us to withstand our trials and tribulations?

Lastly, do we use the gift He has given us? God didn't just bring salvation to us for us not to share it with the rest of the world. God saved your life so that you could share the gift of eternal life with others! This gift came at a high price. Higher than anything we can buy here. Value the most precious gift of all.

Journal

Day 7

Take time to meditate on God's word. What's on your heart this week?

_____

_____

_____

_____

_____

_____

_____

_____

_____

_____

_____

_____

_____

_____

_____

_____

_____

_____

_____

_____

_____

Week Three

Day 1

VICTORY IN JESUS

We were all called to be conquerors.

"I have said these things to you, that in me you may have peace. In the world you will have tribulation. But take heart; I have overcome the world." John 16:33

God tells us that in Him we have peace and that He knows we will fall short, but He has overcome all our shortcomings. If He has overcome the world, and He lives inside of us, we can have hope that we will overcome our sins.

We have been called to conquer. We have been called to overcome. We have been called because He has already fought the world and won. Our battles are His and they have already been claimed victorious.

We need to claim victory over our sins.

We win when we choose God!

Day 2

MEDITATE ON HIS WORD

Make sure you are meditating on His word.

Have you ever thought about meditation? Not the "kumbaya" fingers-together type of meditation, but the meditation that God wants you to have with Him over scripture, the friendship that He longs to have with you through praise. God is always seeking a better relationship with us. One way to strengthen our relationship with God is by taking a verse or a song, just something that God has laid on your heart, and meditating over it. Then just allow it to fill you, allow it to overwhelm you in His presence. Allow it to really sink in and cause a reaction from Him within your life.

God is a God of reaction. He wants to move within you so that you can feel His presence. He is a giving God wanting to give to you.

Try meditating on His word and see what He can show you through it!

I lie awake thinking of you, meditating on you through the night.
Because you are my helper, I sing for joy in the shadow of your wings. I
cling to you; your strong right hand holds me securely.
Psalm 63:6-8 (NLT)

Day 3

LIVING IN THE IN-BETWEEN

Jesus answered, "Even if I do bear witness about myself, my testimony is true, for I know where I come from and where I am going, but you do not know where I come from or where I am going." John 8:14

In this scripture Jesus is addressing the Pharisees about their lack of faith. If you read through until verse thirty, you will see that Jesus spoke with them with such truth and light that many come to believe in Him. I love the confidence this scripture teaches us to have. "For I know where I come from and where I am going." Do you know where you come from and where you are going?

This is important for us to know. Our testimony is our witness of God's faithfulness in our lives. We are to bear witness to what He has done and continues to do. We are to walk in confidence and testify the many works He has performed over our lives. This is the truth and the light of who we live with and live for. He is the light of the world. He who has created us is truth and will never leave us alone. We are created from God and are living for Him.

"And he who sent me is with me. He has not left me alone, for I always do the things that are pleasing to him."
John 8:29

When we know where we come from and where we are going, we then know what our job is to do in the in-between. Live fully in your in-between testifying our God's faithfulness!

Day 4

MORE THAN ENOUGH

Have mercy on me, O God, according to your steadfast love; according to your abundant mercy blot out my transgressions. Wash me thoroughly from my iniquity, and cleanse me from my sin! For I know my transgressions, and my sin is ever before me. Against you, you only, have I sinned and done what is evil in your sight, so that you may be justified in your words and blameless in your judgement. Behold, I was brought forth in iniquity, and in sin did my mother conceive me. Behold, you delight in truth in the inward being, and you teach me wisdom in the secret heart. Psalm 51:1-6

God's words are a story that He tells generation to generation. God's plans are far better than our own! He gets all the glory. It is never about us. What matters is what's inside of you. God never writes us off; He is always redeeming. Nothing disqualifies us from the love of God! We plan a course for our lives, but only the Lord can determine our steps. God is the giver of our dreams and desires, but His way of getting us there is how He straightens our paths. He can put us in far better places than we can put ourselves. The gifts God has given you are more than enough. You are more than enough!

Trust! We allow others' perceptions of us to determine who we are, but God creates in us a clean heart. We weren't created for others; we were created for God! All of our stories, our sins, our flaws…he takes all of those things and creates a masterpiece. He creates a canvas covered in grace. Everyone's story matters. God isn't a God after perfection. He isn't a God after a flawless performance. He just wants us to trust Him. He wants us to be honest and not to try to fix ourselves without Him. Be you! Be the beautiful image

God created only you to be. God can see your complete story, whereas you can only see it in pieces. God uses it all to tell a better story of your life and of who He is. God doesn't need you. He wants you!

What He has given us is more than enough.

Day 5

YOU ARE WORTHY

A lot of times we get tied to things that are not in the hands of God. When we tie ourselves to those things, God is unable to use us where He wants us. When we break down those ties and allow Him to open doors, we can be turned in the direction of God's plans.

When we allow God to move, we allow blessings.

Have you ever felt tied to your past? My past made me feel unworthy. What I had done, the mistakes I had made, the people I chose to be a part of my life…all of it just made me feel like I wasn't worthy to do anything big enough for God. What I didn't realize, though, is that God loves to call those who believe they aren't worthy. God wants to take the mess and use it to extend His Kingdom. Your mess could be someone else's blessing.

We don't need to tie ourselves down to things that aren't of God. We can't allow ourselves to be tied to sin and to God. God doesn't want us to view ourselves as any less valuable than the way He views us.

So God created man in his own image, in the image of God he created
him; male and female he created them.
Genesis 1:27

If all of who we are — our flaws, our insecurities, our mistakes, and our failures — were created in the image of God, how could we not be worthy enough?

Day 6

STAY FOCUSED ON THE CALLING

Fixing our eyes on Jesus, the pioneer and perfecter of faith. For the joy set before him he endured the cross, scorning its shame, and has sat down at the right hand of the throne of God. Hebrews 12:2 (NIV)

We must view God just as He is. That may just be the first step in accepting Him for what He can do. When we are focused on Him as our leader, we can understand that we are nothing but His followers. He is the driver of our car, and we are just merely passengers. He takes us where we are supposed to go, but we always have the option to stop Him and take over ourselves. He gives us free will. He still loves you enough to continue the journey with you, but the journey may be a little different when you are behind the wheel and He isn't.

Focus on the Calling. God wants to direct our paths. He wants to lead us by still waters. He wants us to stay focused on His love, what He has done for us, and what He has called us to do so that we can gather His harvest in our lives.

Journal

Day 7

Take time to meditate on God's word. What's on your heart this week?

_____

_____

_____

_____

_____

_____

_____

_____

_____

_____

_____

_____

_____

_____

_____

_____

_____

_____

_____

Week Four

Day 1

JUMP OFF THE HAMPSTER WHEEL

For God gave us a spirit not of fear but of power and love and self-control. 2 Timothy 1:7

Satan tries to hold us down with fear. He is the one who tells us we're not good enough. He reminds us of our pasts and tries make us feel incapable of spreading God's word.

Fear isn't from God. He is about power and sound mind. When we fear, we allow Satan to keep us from what God has called us to do.

Fear can be a cycle. You can decide to jump off of it or stay stuck in it. Cycles just repeat themselves over and over again. It's like a broken record.

A lot of us get caught up in cycles and think this is it. This is all we were planted here for. God has called us for nothing more than this right now. God does want us to live in our now's, but He also has called us for more than the cycles we can begin to find ourselves in.

God didn't plan our lives to be revolving doors. Satan planted the cycle of "no more." God wants way more!

Don't hold yourself down with fear, unable to walk in faith. God has called you to step out in faith, to stop hitting the repeat button, and to jump off that hamster wheel. God called you for a path He paved. Stop being gripped with fear and instead get gripped within His word.

Day 2

WORDS STICK LIKE HONEY

Words can be so harsh. It's amazing how some things we say can make someone's day, and other things can cut them like a sword.

Telling lies about others is as harmful as hitting them with an ax, wounding them with a sword, or shooting them with a sharp arrow.
Proverbs 25:18 (NLT)

Even when we are upset, words are not to be used haphazardly. The words we say are like honey. They stick to people and can create setbacks in one's ability to feel wanted, to trust others, or to love themselves. We are not here to push others down; we are here to build them up.

Let no corrupting talk come out of your mouths, but only such as is good for building up, as fits the occasion, that it may give grace to those who hear. Ephesians 4:29

When we choose kindness to those who choose something else to us, we are choosing God. It's not easy to always show kindness when we feel hurt or threatened. However, we should be gentle, caring, and humble like God was when his enemies shamed Him and nailed Him to a cross.

Your kindness will reward you, but your cruelty will destroy you.
Proverbs 11:17 (NLT)

When using hurtful, condemning words toward someone, you're only creating boundaries within yourself. God has called everyone His, so who are we to claim these words over someone else? As much as we may feel like saying

something hurtful, we need to check our hearts. The hurt may be coming from a place we need to be seeking God for comfort and deliverance from. We need to focus on building others up.

Day 3

WHAT HE LONGS FOR

Life sure does throw us some huge curve balls at times. It seems like we get hit with some of those balls repeatedly. Like the saying, "When it rains, it pours." Thankfully, we serve a God that has promised his refuge in hard times. He's promised to shield us and to be our stronghold during those times in our life.

Hear my cry, O God, listen to my prayer; from the end of the earth I call to you when my heart is faint. Lead me to the rock that is higher than I, for you have been my refuge, a strong tower against the enemy. Let me dwell in your tent forever! Let me take refuge under the shelter of your wings! Psalm 61:1-4

The God we serve is an everlasting God. Unlike us, He doesn't grow weary. When we feel overwhelmed with the pressures of life, God has called us to find comfort within Him. He is higher than any storm we could face. Higher than cancer! Higher than our marital issues! Higher than financial problems! Higher than any addiction! God wants to be your shelter. He is here to be used. When you use Him for comfort and shelter, you are drawing nearer to Him. That's the relationship He longs for with you.

Day 4

BEAUTY FROM ASHES

God is always refining us as his children. He's always shaping and molding us into who He wants us to be for Him. Just like a silversmith, God is not done until He can see His reflection in us.

The words of the Lord are pure words, as silver tried in a furnace on the ground, purified seven times. Psalm 12:6

We are just like a piece of metal. We are burned and tried in life. With each burn we are shaped into something more. We are cleaned up and re-purposed in God's word.

God is always taking exactly what we think may do us in and turning it into something that is going to purify us.

He will give a crown of beauty for ashes.
Isaiah 61:3 (NLT)

Day 5

LET US THANK HIM

Today, let us thank Him. Let's give thanks to the One who has supplied for us over and more abundantly than we deserve. He has filled us with a love that surpasses any earthly love. He has embraced, cleansed, and set us free from all our mistakes. Let's be thankful.

And whatever you do, in word or deed, do everything in the name of the Lord Jesus, giving thanks to God the Father through him.
Colossians 3:17

It's so easy to want God to show up and then not give him thanks when we think He doesn't. We forget that God never goes anywhere. A lot of times it's us that loses Him. Our God is a God who deserves thanks and praise through all things and through all times.

Being thankful and giving thanks truly blesses His heart. When we want to continually be blessed, do we think about the blessings He has already bestowed upon us?

Let's bless Him today with thanks for everything He has done and has yet to do!

Give thanks in all circumstances.
1 Thessalonians 5:18

Day 6

POWER OF PRAYER

In the morning, Lord, you hear my voice; in the morning I lay my requests before you and wait expectantly.
Psalm 5:3 (NIV)

We always need to pray for others—pray for others to have spiritual strength in Christ. Growing in God and our faith through prayer makes us stronger in our belief.

We tend to think that our prayer life is supposed to happen before bed. That's how I grew up anyway. You pray before meals and going to sleep. Prayer, though, is a lot more than just mealtime and bedtime. Prayer is always. It should be constant. Praying gives you a closer connection to the One above.

God wants us to rely on Him as if He were always physically with us. He wants to show us that a deeper connection to Him comes in the power of prayer. Prayer is something that brings you closer to Him on a deeper level. When we cry, seek Him, and open our hearts, that's when we reach a vulnerable place for Him to speak to us.

Journal

Day 7

Take time to meditate on God's word. What's on your heart this week?

_____

_____

_____

_____

_____

_____

_____

_____

_____

_____

_____

_____

_____

_____

_____

_____

_____

_____

_____

Week Five

Day 1

ALPHA & OMEGA

Where does God stand in your life? Is He in the front or closer to the sidelines? Do you go to Him first when you need something, or are you quicker to go to someone or something else?

God wants to be first! He wants to be the first you go to when you are having a bad day at work or when you just need help through a tough time. He wants to be the first when you feel like you've failed as a parent or when you have lost a loved one. When you wake up in the morning until you go to sleep at night, God wants to be your beginning and your end. No matter the circumstance or the degree of the issue, God wants to take precedence over anyone or anything.

I have set the Lord always before me; because he is at my right hand, I will not be shaken.
Psalm 16:8

God should be our right-hand man.

He wants to be the first one you run to. He is the only one that can deliver you. God longs to have the type of relationship with you that even though He already knows it all, you still present it to Him as if He knows nothing at all. He wants to know His place is on the platform lifted higher than anyone else.

When He is on the platform, we are not moved.

Day 2

UNPACK HIS SCRIPTURE

There have many times in my life I have been unprepared. I have felt very unequipped, but God has always shined His light even in my darkest hours. Did you know that God's word is supposed to be stored within your heart? In both our biggest celebratory times and darkest times, God's word is to have the biggest impact. You know how we store all our Christmas decorations away for a season? As Christmas comes back around, we begin to unpack it again. God's word is supposed to be the very same, and it's not just capable of being used in one season. His word can be used through all seasons.

As seasons come and go in our lives, God wants us to have His word stored up so that we can begin to unpack it in our times of need, desperation, or just in our sweet everyday life.

His word was never intended to be read and forgotten. His word was intended to be placed safely and securely within us. It was intended to be used as a weapon of safety. It was intended for armor.

As this year comes to an end and a new year begins, we will start to think of resolutions. This year I would like for all of you to join me in memorizing scriptures to store inside our hearts. Scriptures that can be used to unpack truth and light into our lives. Let's store as much of God's word as we can!

I have stored up your word in my heart,
that I might not sin against you.
Psalm 119:11

Day 3

DRINK FROM HIS WELL

The lady of Samaria first doubted Jesus, then believed in who He was, and then influenced others with her belief.

That's very similar to our own stories as we come to Christ and then build our relationship with Him.

"Everyone who drinks of this water will be thirsty again, but whoever drinks of the water I give them will never be thirsty again."
John 4:13-14

When we get drunk off worldly things, we continue to thirst for more. However, when we drink from the well of God, He takes away the thirst for anything of this world and just keeps us thirsty for more of Him.

The lady in Samaria doubted Jesus, but when she allowed herself to take in more of Him, she realized who He was and what He could do. We must be more willing to let Him in through word and through truth.

The lady of Samaria was a testimony to others. When she went back and told all the others about Jesus and what He had shown her, that's when others started coming to Christ. Jesus gives us what we need to be able to give others what they need. Through us they can receive the best gift of all, and that's a relationship with Jesus Christ.

Day 4

ENDLESS POSSIBILITIES

But Peter rose and ran to the tomb; stooping and looking in, he saw the linen cloths by themselves; and he went home marveling at what had happened. Luke 24:12

Has God ever done something for you that made you marvel at what happened? In this verse Jesus had risen from the tomb just as God had promised it would happen.

I can remember a time when I would marvel at the fact that I owned my own home. I would pull out of the driveway and look back at it and just thank God for how he had moved in my life. It was simply all because of how He loved me and promised that He'd take care of me. It was such a blessing. He always promises to take care of His children.

Peter knew what He was capable of. We do too. We serve a God with endless possibilities who loves us more than we can comprehend.

Take some time today and just marvel at the ways God has worked in your life. Ponder the small and big ways he has moved in your life. He has walked with you, cared for you, and fulfilled promises that without Him couldn't be fulfilled.

Thank Him for being your Father and have a grateful heart today.

Day 5

CONFESS YOUR SINS

"As I live, says the Lord, every knee shall bow to me, and every tongue shall confess to God."
Romans 14:11

Even though our God knows the things we do, we still have to confess them to Him for Him to begin to restore us. Sin can consume us and that leaves no room for God in our heart. When we confess our sins, God is then able to do a multitude of things inside of us so that we can remove what consumes us and is not of Him.

1. Deliverance - When you confess your sins, God can help you overcome them. You must make the first step, which is to know that what you have done is not right. When you step out to ask God for deliverance from what you've done, he can begin to remove it.

2. Forgiveness - Confessing sin is confessing your heart to God. It's becoming vulnerable and wanting help. God can forgive you for the things you have done and then begin to work on your heart, so you do not want to continue to do sinful things but want to live a life for Him.

3. Healing - When we confess our sins to God, He isn't just helping deliver us, He is also helping to heal us from our sinful nature. God wants to give us restoration and peace. He wants us to be able to change our ways into His ways. Confess your sinful ways to God. Don't allow your sins to burden and weigh you down. Let God take complete residence inside your heart.

Day 6

THE HARVEST WILL COME

We all fall apart! We know that God wants us to fall into him when we are broken and distraught. God also wants us to pick ourselves up and fight! He doesn't want us to stay down. Usually, when we believe in something and want something bad enough, we fight for it.

When you really want a job, you work for it. When you want to win at a sport, you practice. When you need to get in shape, you go to the gym and start eating healthier. The problem is that a lot of us work on so many things around us that we give up on what's right in front of us.

God wants us to fight for our marriages. He wants us to fight for our kids. He wants us to fight *inside* of our homes before we deplete our energy *outside* of them.

And let us not grow weary of doing good, for in due season we will reap, if we do not give up.
Galatians 6:9

Don't give up on what God has handed you. Sometimes life gets tough. Your kids may become disobedient. Your marriage may seem like it's failing. But God says when we keep pushing forward, when we continue to do what we know is right, and when we seek him and stay diligent in our faith, the harvest will come.

Don't Give Up!

Journal

Day 7

Take time to meditate on God's word. What's on your
heart this week?

_____

_____

_____

_____

_____

_____

_____

_____

_____

_____

_____

_____

_____

_____

_____

_____

_____

_____

_____

Week Six

Day 1

PLANT YOUR TREASURES

When we leave this earth, others are left with what we leave behind: the relationships we build, the morals we instill, and what we choose to do with our lives for the short period God gives us here on earth. God gives us our lives here to touch others, to speak to others, and to share God's word.

He sets us apart in our mother's womb. What we do here is what we choose as our legacy for others to remember and pass down to the next generation.

Some people's impacts fade with time, while others leave a lasting impact for years to come.

When we go to be with our Heavenly Father, we want to be remembered by what set us apart. We want to be remembered as always following Jesus and living a life that was used to minister to others through the Holy Spirit. Our legacy here is important because it should represent Christ. If what we do always points to Jesus then it doesn't matter if we are remembered at all, just as long as He is.

Where your treasure is, there your heart will be also.
Matthew 6:21

Where we spend our time and what we do with it while we are here show where our treasure lies. When God calls us home, we want to make sure that our hearts were in the right place. I challenge you to sit down and list out all the places you find your treasure.

Day 2

REMAIN CONSISTENT

God honors consistency.

Consistency with God will bring you closer to Him.

When we are consistent with God - with our Bible reading and our prayer life - we begin to be less reliant on ourselves and others and more on Him.

Jesus Christ is the same yesterday and today and forever.
Hebrews 13:8 (NIV)

Nothing changes with the One above.

- We change.
- We become less motivated.
- We stop praying.
- We stop seeking Him out.
- We quit relying on Him and begin to focus on ourselves.
- Neither God nor the Son of God ever changes.
- Who they are and their love for us remain the same every day; they never falter.

God wants us to stay consistent, to commit to learning His word, and to establish a prayer life so that He can begin to unravel His great plans.

Consistency is key.

Day 3

POWERLESS WITHOUT HIM

*But he said to me, "My grace is sufficient for you, for my power is
made perfect in weakness."*
2 Corinthians 12:9 (NIV)

He gives strength to the weary and increases the power of the weak.
Isaiah 40:29 (NIV)

Finally, be strong in the Lord and in his mighty power.
Ephesians 6:10 (NIV)

God's power is so intense and so strong that it can't be
described in words. All three of these scriptures have a
common word, "power." Nothing has power without God.

All of those things that seem like they are weighing you
down have no power without God. Nothing can be broken
without the power of God. You may give worry, addiction,
fear, and defeat the power to hold you down, those things
have no power compared to God's.

If you don't have God's power over you, you have nothing.
His name is the only name that should hold power over us.
Nothing has any power to stand against us unless it was
formed within Him. God holds all the power.

But in that coming day no weapon turned against you will succeed.
You will silence every voice raised up to accuse you. These benefits are
enjoyed by the servants of the Lord. Isaiah 54:17 (NLT)

Day 4

HE IS MORE THAN A TEMPORARY FIX

When we submit ourselves to the Lord, He produces change.

A lot of times, we do exactly what we want to do. When we don't have what we want, we will go out and buy it. We may put it on credit and then end up in debt. We alter our bodies to satisfy our minds. We establish relationships that aren't healthy because we think that's what we want.

Submit yourselves therefore to God. Resist the devil, and he will flee from you. Draw near to God, and he will draw near to you.
James 4:7-8

We all want some sort of change, but we don't realize that the change we really need is inside our hearts. We think that once we buy that thing or get in that relationship, we will be happy, but what we fail to see is that the only thing that will truly make us happy isn't of this world.

God is the change you need to fill the voids.

Trying to fill a void with temporary things will never truly satisfy you.

You will only be truly satisfied when you have a relationship and connection with Jesus Christ.

That is not a temporary thing. He is forever.

Day 5

ULTILIZE YOUR TIME

We waste a lot of time on things that don't matter. The devil comes in and tries to steal our joy with the words someone says or the things we wish we were doing. We allow ourselves to be consumed by the negative, and we let our joy be washed away in the time we do have.

Look carefully then how you walk, not as unwise but as wise, making the best use of the time, because the days are evil. Therefore do not be foolish, but understand what the will of the Lord is. Ephesians 5:15-17

How many times have we allowed what someone says to us to take away time from our day because we obsessively worry about it? "Well, that person said this, and now I'm upset and have allowed an hour to go by consuming my brain with why they said it." It doesn't matter what they said or why they said it. What matters is what you're doing with your time. If you're allowing the devil to steal your time with worry, then you won't be able to utilize it for what God has intended it for.

"…making the best use of time because the days are evil." We go about our days wishing we were doing something else and wanting change. We sit back and allow the negative thoughts to take over and dwell inside of us. You can get things done; it's all in how you make use of what you have. Quit allowing the things that don't matter to take up time that you won't ever get back. Don't allow your time to be depleted with things that don't matter, *"…but understand what the will of the Lord is.*

Day 6

ENGRAVED IN HIS HANDS

Monogramming has been a craze for a while. At least I know it has been in the South. We get everything monogrammed, from our jackets to our kids' shoes. We want everyone to know what three letters our parents decided to mark us with when we were born. I'm not going to lie, it's cute, and I may have a few necklaces with my kids' initials on them.

You know what the Lord says in Isaiah 49:16?

"Behold, I have engraved you on the palms of my hands."

When we have Jesus, He doesn't mark us on a piece of clothing or jewelry, He marks us on himself. He engraves us inside of Him. When He was pierced with the nails, He was pierced with our transgressions. We are engraved on Him.

We are His statement, His distinctive piece to go into the world and show who He is.

We have been monogrammed in the palms of His hands.

Nothing and nobody can tell us who or what we are. He has already engraved that on Himself. He knows what we have been called for. He wants us to be a statement for Him in the world.

Journal

Day 7

Take time to meditate on God's word. What's on your heart this week?

_____

_____

_____

_____

_____

_____

_____

_____

_____

_____

_____

_____

_____

_____

_____

_____

_____

_____

_____

Week Seven

Day 1

DOUBTING THOMAS

After the resurrection Jesus appeared to the disciples. One of the twelve, Thomas, wasn't with the others when Jesus came. Thomas wouldn't believe it unless he saw it for himself. He wanted to see His nail driven hands, and he wanted to be able to touch them. Eight days after Jesus came back, He gave Thomas the opportunity to touch His hands. This is what Jesus says to Thomas,

"Put your finger here, and see my hands; and put out your hand, and place it in my side. Do not disbelieve, but believe." Thomas then answered him, "My Lord and my God!" Jesus said to him, "Have you believed because you have seen me? Blessed are those who have not seen and yet have believed." John 20:27-29

Are you a doubter? How much do you truly believe in His power and presence? When we pray, we need to believe in the power of that prayer. Our God is real, and our God delivers. We may not be able to see how God is moving or is going to move, but we must believe in the movement.

Don't be a doubter!

"Blessed are those who have not seen and yet still believe."

Day 2

GET UP

In John 5:6, healing is about to take place on the Sabbath. Jesus walked up to a man and asked,

> *"Do you want to be healed?" The sick man answered him, "Sir, I have no one to put me into the pool when the water is stirred up, and while I am going another steps down before me." Jesus said to him, "Get up, take up your bed, and walk." John 5:6-8*

What excuses are you making to not follow God and do what He is laying on your heart? There is healing that needs to take place within you and for your life.

Don't let the healing slip by because you're afraid to take the step! Sometimes it's in our obedience that God is beginning to heal us.

You may be fighting the same problem for years. This man fought his sickness for 38 years. You might start wondering where your healing is.

Don't look for it in your excuses; it will never be found.

Take shelter under the One who can make you walk again. God has claimed the victory over your healing. Just as Jesus said to this man, *"Get up,"* we must get up. He wants us to claim Jesus' power over our healing and walk.

Then He says to sin no more!

Day 3

TAKE DOWN THE BARRIERS

Did you know that God puts no barriers on how close we can get to him? It's all up to us. He knows our inner depths, and He longs for us to want to know the inner depths of who He is. He wants us to know him at such a deep level that when we feel our connection faltering, we become concerned and long for more of Him.

More of a relationship
More desire to serve
More prayer
More scripture
More quiet time
More of a connection

We get to choose how close we live to Him. The only roadblocks we have with Him are the ones we put up. When we go our way instead of His, that is a detour we decided to take. Our detour could be why we are experiencing so much conflict. There is nothing stopping us from a relationship with God other than ourselves.

For I am sure that neither death nor life, nor angels nor rulers, nor things present nor things to come, nor powers, nor height nor depth, nor anything else in all creation, will be able to separate us from the love of God in Christ Jesus our Lord. Romans 8:38-39

Nothing we do can separate us from the love He has for us. What barriers do you need to tear down today so that you can begin to have a deeper connection with Him?

Day 4

DON'T STOP EXTENDING

There are just some people that no matter how many times you keep extending that olive branch, it seems like you get the same outcome over and over. You keep hoping for something different, but you continue to be disappointed. There is no footing to stand with them.

Imagine Noah in his ark, surrounded by water, trusting the Lord that He would bring him to dry land, wanting to be grounded again. He sent a dove out to see if the waters had subsided from the earth. The dove came back because she found nowhere to set her feet down.

There is always hope for change. God still wants us to trust in Him and continue to extend our hands to others with the same grace that we have been given from Him.

Noah then waited another seven days and again sent the dove out of the ark. This time, the dove came back with a freshly picked olive leaf. Noah then knew the waters had subsided. Noah allowed his faith to be bigger than his fear. He knew that God promised deliverance. We also have to trust in the process.

Sometimes, even though it may not seem like things are changing, we have to continue to seek the change.

Then he waited another seven days and sent forth the dove, and she did not return to him anymore.
Genesis 8:12

If there is one thing we should know, it's that we serve a

God who always delivers what He has promised. I believe we must, just as Noah did, trust in God's process. We must continue to release the dove hoping for change, God's change! Even in those times that change may not come when we want it or the way we had hoped it would, we still need to remember that God's hands are on every situation. Be hopeful and fervent in spirit and know that with whatever outcome of extending that branch, God will always prevail.

Day 5

DEEP SECRETS

Don't we all have some things tucked away, deeply planted that we've either tried so hard to forget or would rather not talk about? Think of your deepest secret. The one that you've tucked down so far, or the one you're ashamed to let anyone know about.

Release it.

Every secret you've ever put away. Every secret you've planned to forget about, God knows and still loves you.

The secret things belong to the Lord our God, but the things that are revealed belong to us and to our children forever, that we may do all the words of this law. Deuteronomy 29:29

Everything we are and have been; our past, our present, and even our future belong to God. What has been revealed through His word belongs to us.

Don't be ashamed. Don't feel guilty, and don't waste another day being stuck in your secrets. Repent and give them to God.

Day 6

THE NEXT GENERATION

We have a responsibility to the next generation. As parents, as leaders, and as Christians, we are called to instill values in these kids who are rising to be Christ followers.

These days, kids are becoming bogged down with more pressure than ever before. They are exposed to harsher worldly sin that has become "fingertip" accessible. With the world being so influential on today's kids and their self-confidence being depleted, we must be ready to defend them from Satan and show God to them. As adults, what we allow to consume us has an obvious effect. When we eat too much food, we gain weight. When we read our Bible, pray, and start to immerse ourselves in the word, we grow closer to Christ. It sounds simple, but to kids it's not so apparent. They need us to show them what Christ-like favor looks like! For us to do that, we must remain diligent in seeking the word ourselves. They are our responsibility. We must invest in what God puts in front of us.

Jesus said,

> *"The thief comes only to steal and kill and destroy. I came that they may have life and have it abundantly."*
> *John 10:10*

Satan wants nothing more than to bind our children with sin. That's why we need to remain consistent in showing and teaching them about God. Claiming God's power and image over our children begins to remove the lies that the enemy can create. Power is in the constant. Make God the constant!

Journal

Day 7

Take time to meditate on God's word. What's on your heart this week?

_____

_____

_____

_____

_____

_____

_____

_____

_____

_____

_____

_____

_____

_____

_____

_____

_____

_____

_____

_____

_____

_____

Week Eight

Day 1

PROOF IS IN HIS NAME

In John 4:46-54, a man hears that Jesus is coming and goes to Jesus asking Him to heal his son because he was at the point of death. Jesus says this to the man:

"Unless you see signs and wonders you will not believe." John 4:48

The man in this scripture wanted healing for his son but needed Jesus to confirm who He was so that he could believe. He was a doubter.

We are sometimes the same way. We want God to give us a sign - show us proof so that we can believe in what He can do. Why can't we just believe?

Confirmation can be significant, but a faith that doesn't need it can be influential. Sometimes God is just calling us to believe and have faith in knowing what He can do. It's nothing more than just knowing exactly whom we serve.

*The official said to him, "Sir, come down before my child dies." Jesus said to him, "Go; your son will live." The man believed the word that Jesus spoke to him and went on his way. As he was going down, his servants met him and told him that his son was recovering. So he asked them the hour when he began to get better, and they said to him, "Yesterday at the seventh hour the fever left him." The father knew that was the hour when Jesus had said to him, "Your son will live." And he himself believed, and all his household. This was now the second sign that Jesus did when he had come from Judea to Galilee.
John 4:49-54*

God wants us to know without doubting what His ability is to provide for us. We must believe in what He can do without needing the proof before He does it. The proof is already there. He sent his Son to die for us to give us eternal life. The promise is written throughout the Bible. He rose again. The proof is in the power of His name.

Day 2

FINISHING WITH GROWTH

Because you know that the testing of your faith produces perseverance.
James 1:3 (NIV)

I've always heard, "Don't pray for patience because you may not like what He puts you through to learn it." The truth is that when your faith is tested, it produces the patience within you to withstand the test. When we start to understand that the test isn't always a bad thing, that it allows us to grow, we can choose to grow in the right direction.

We know that in life we will be tested. Sometimes tests can come more than once a day, and they may seem to never end. God wants to develop our character. He isn't a God who hurts us; He is a God who wants us to be complete within Him.

Next time you undergo a test, pray for God to give you the endurance to finish it. Finishing first isn't important but finishing with growth is. When we finish with growth, we are allowing ourselves to become closer to the One who can truly withstand all tests.

If you are going through a test today, ask God for the endurance to finish the race at His speed. Remember, He does all things with purpose.

Day 3

FAITH OVER FEAR

Do you truly know just how powerful our God is? When you're in the midst of hard times, you just want to give up, and you start questioning where He is in your storm, you are placing your fear over your faith. You are allowing Satan to overpower the hand of God in your circumstance.

Most of us have been there, and if you haven't, you will be. We tend to question the ability of God when the storm hits. We can begin to wonder how powerful and mighty He really is when we are in the midst of it. The storm can be blinding and cause us to forget His abilities. It becomes easier to forget the further away we are from Him, but listen to what God can do:

> *And when he got into the boat, his disciples followed him. And behold, there arose a great storm on the sea, so that the boat was being swamped by the waves; but he was asleep. And they went and woke him, saying, "Save us, Lord; we are perishing." And he said to them, "Why are you afraid, O you of little faith?" Then he rose and rebuked the winds and the sea, and there was a great calm. And the men marveled, saying, "What sort of man is this, that even winds and sea obey him?"*
> *Matthew 8:23-27*

How many times do we cry out to God asking Him to save us, to fix our problems, to help us? This makes me wonder how many times God has looked at us and said, "O you of little faith." I don't know about you, but I want my faith to overpower my fears.

I want to know my God is bigger than any storm. To truly

feel that, we have to feel Him. We must get close to Him.

"What sort of man is this, that even winds and sea obey him?" Our God is a God of great power. If even the wind and seas obey him, so will I.

Day 4

LET US LOVE

Dear friends, let us love one another, for love comes from God.
Everyone who loves has been born of God and knows God. Whoever
does not love does not know God, because God is love.
1 John 4:7-8 (NIV)

Love is such a small word with a complex meaning. How do we fill a world with love when a lot of the world has never known true love? You have had first loves, puppy love, and even the love you share with your family, spouse, and children, but do you really know love?

To know love is to know God, for God is love. Do you know the love of God? God's love for us is unfailing, unfaltering, and flawless. His love is complete and remains complete. When He sent His Son to die on the cross, the promise was that three days later He would be resurrected. On that day He marked it complete.

Let all you do be done in love.
1 Corinthians 16:14

To love the way Christ loves, we must first love Him! God wants the love that we share with others to be the same flawless love He shares with us. He wants our love to be so profound in Him others come seeking the same love.

Love is giving, not self-seeking. Love is kind, not judgmental. Love is a free gift. When we truly know the love of God, then the love of God projects through us. Let us love!

Day 5

LOSE THE WORLD & PROFIT HIM

We tend to forget that when we want a life full of Jesus, we must let go of a life full of us! We like to live our lives full of the things we want. We want new cars because the one we have isn't good enough. We want a new house because the one we have isn't big enough. We want more money. We buy more toys. We consume ourselves with our worldly desires instead of our needs. What we fail to realize is that our need is Jesus, and Jesus came free. Instead of accepting that and living with just the need for Christ, we temporarily fill our voids by fulfilling our desires. Then we just move on to wanting something else new. New is always nice when it's new, but just like the last thing, it will get old. The replacements keep coming because the void was never truly filled.

For instance, your marriage may not be new anymore, but is the problem really your relationship, or is it you? Is your heart just not where it's supposed to be? It may be time to let go of the things that aren't helping your walk with God.

We need to get in the mindset where we know what is of God and what is not. All things on earth will just be ash when He comes back. Those things, those people, and that vacation all seem nice now, but what are you doing gaining the whole world and losing your soul?

God can't do anything with things, God does things with you! He wants you all the time the way you want Him when things are bad.

We profit nothing if we gain these temporary things in this world, and we lose our souls while doing it. You must fix your eyes on God. God gives you what you need when you need it. Quit worrying about the new best thing.

"If anyone would come after me, let him deny himself and take up his cross and follow me."
Mark 8:34

Day 6

SURRENDER THE WEIGHT

What weight are you carrying today?

The weight could be from something that happened all the way back in your childhood. It could be from something you blame yourself for. It could be the death of someone close to you, a mistake you made, or a decision you had to make that just didn't pan out the way you thought it would. I want to tell you, though, that God doesn't want a burden to claim the victory He has for us. Our burdens weren't meant to weigh us down; we serve a God that wants to lighten our load!

Cast your burden on the Lord, and he shall sustain you; he shall never permit the righteous to be moved. Psalm 55:22

What's the first thing that comes to mind when you hear cast? Fishing? That's exactly what I thought. When we cast out our line, we are hoping to bring back something big. We pray for that massive fish. You know, the one you can later brag about. Just like when we cast out our lines, God wants us to cast out our burdens and let them go. When we cast Him the burdens that are weighing us down, He wants us to reel back something called freedom.

"Come to me, all who labor and are heavy laden, and I will give you rest. Take my yoke upon you, and learn from me, for I am gentle and lowly in heart, and you will find rest for your souls. For my yoke is easy, and my burden is light."
Matthew 11:28-30

The burden that's causing you to be weighed down is

exactly what God is calling you to drop. Some things are bigger than us. They are not meant for us, they are meant for the One who can deliver us. We must surrender the weight. God can't begin to move until you give Him what He needs to carry.

What's in your backpack that needs to be moved to His? Stop trying to carry what His hands are supposed to hold. Don't allow your burden to weigh you down and keep you from the blessing that God wants to deliver to you. Make room for His blessing. Cast it out, and let it go.

Journal

Day 7

Take time to meditate on God's word. What's on your heart this week?

_____

_____

_____

_____

_____

_____

_____

_____

_____

_____

_____

_____

_____

_____

_____

_____

_____

_____

_____

_____

_____

_____

Week Nine

Day 1

FIRST PRIORITY

"Whoever can be trusted with very little can also be trusted with much." Luke 16:10 (NIV)

Do you want more? Do you have a dream or goal you want to live out for God? If so, He's calling you to be obedient in your walk. Maybe He's calling you to be more consistent in prayer and to spend more alone time with Him each day. Are you making Him your first priority, or are you putting other things first and running out of time for Him?

How can God trust you with your dream if you can't even make time for Him? If He knows you can't be obedient in the present, why would he trust you in the future? God wants us to show what we can be trusted with.

If we want to trust in Him, why shouldn't He be able to trust in us?

He wants to know that we are devoted to doing the little things that grow His kingdom so that He can entrust us with the bigger things. He has more for us. More than just going to church on some Sundays and praying when we find the time. He has so much more He would like to share with you, but He is waiting to see what you do with the little before He reveals "the big."

Stay obedient!

Day 2

BEND DOWN

Jesus loves to teach. Jesus was God and therefore knew what man would do, but in order to teach or make a point, He asked questions as if He didn't. John 8 tells of the woman who was caught in adultery. The scribes and the Pharisees brought the woman to Jesus and told him what she had done.

Jesus bent down and wrote with his finger on the ground. And as they continued to ask him, he stood up and said to them, "Let him who is without sin among you be the first to throw a stone at her." And once more he bent down and wrote on the ground. But when they heard it, they went away one by one, beginning with the older ones, and Jesus was left alone with the woman standing before him. Jesus stood up and said to her, "Woman, where are they? Had no one condemned you?" She said, "No one, Lord." And Jesus said, "Neither do I condemn you: go, and from now on sin no more." John 8:6-11

There is so much to learn from this story of God's grace.

1. We will have people that want to push us down for the things God has already forgiven us for, but Jesus said, "Let him who is without sin among you be the first to throw a stone." No one is without fault and no one can condemn the things you have done but God himself. When we live for God in the now, we don't have to live in the past. We were delivered from the past!

2. Society tells us something different than what God wants us to know. The law commanded that they throw stones at her. Today, society teaches us that if someone does something bad or contradictory to

what society teaches, we are supposed to pick them apart. Forgiveness shouldn't always be offered; second chances are a sign of weakness. God doesn't say that. God says forgiveness is love, and we are to love the way He loves. If He offers the kind of love that is nonjudgmental and freely forgiving, we are to offer it as well.

3. What these men thought would destroy her, Jesus, in this instance, used to resurrect her. You see, they thought they were bringing her to her death, but Jesus had them all walk away one by one as He also showed them what God's grace, mercy, and forgiveness looked like. What you think may be the death of you, God can also use inside of you, to make you rise into who you are supposed to be.

Jesus bent down. Are you bending down to show grace?

Day 3

HE WILL ALWAYS SUPPLY

And my God will supply every need of yours according to his riches in glory in Christ Jesus.
Philippians 4:19

We worry about our future, and we struggle through our days because we allow Satan to have power over what God has already worked out. When we are afraid, we aren't trusting, and when we aren't trusting, we aren't having faith in our Father. God tells us that He will supply every need, not just some. Not just the ones we beg for. Not just the ones we pray about. He said every need. So, the needs you have no idea you even have, He supplies. The needs you prayed over, He supplies. The needs you feel like He has forgotten about...guess what? He will supply.

Are you supplying Him with faith or doubt?

The thing you think you need might be the very thing God has said time and again that you don't. You may also be confusing a "want" for a "need." God may be saying, "Slow down. I have what you need if you'll let me fulfill it. Take a step away from the mindset that 'you know' and step into the mindset of 'He supplies.'"

We don't truly know our own needs the way that He does.

Day 4

ACTION CAUSES REACTION

How do we stand out in a world filled with so many unique styles and different beliefs?

We set out to be who God has created us to be, in His image. However, a lot of times we conform our beliefs to those around us. God chose us to be different. When we stand out, it can cause us to be judged, vulnerable, and even mistreated. When we stand out for Christ we are becoming like Christ. Our actions shouldn't represent what the world is doing, but what Christ is doing through us.

We should want to stand out, so that others can join in. Our whole objective in being whom Christ has called us to be is to direct others to Him.

In the same way, let your light shine before others, so that they may see your good works and give glory to your Father who is in heaven.
Matthew 5:16

When we blend in, we miss opportunities God has for us. It takes steps of faith in standing out to walk in the direction of God. Blending in comes easy because you can hide in others' footsteps. We can get lost in other people's callings and miss our own. We weren't meant to walk in anyone's footsteps but God's.

To stand out you will have to get uncomfortable. People will need to see your light shine. An action causes a reaction. Could you imagine your light being the cause of other lights beginning to shine?

Day 5

HIS LOVE SURROUNDS US

It's good to be reminded of God's love. We tend to forget just how great it is and how much we need it. We wonder how we can comprehend a love so profound as the love God has for us. Is it humanly possible to understand a love so deep? God's love can't be measured. His love for us is so abundant that we must experience it.

How can you experience God's love? You can begin to experience it through prayer, through hard times, through reading your bible, and through seeking him. God's love for us is the most authentic thing in our lives. Long after the world is gone and nothing remains, His love will endure.

Give thanks to the God of heaven, for his steadfast love endures forever. Psalm 136:26

God's love never ends and never changes. We must not allow ourselves to forget how true His love is. It's always the same today, yesterday and tomorrow. When we have Jesus in our hearts, we will always have the love of God, a love that allows us to be who we are. A love that is eternal.

Are we choosing God's love over the world? Do we live as if we know that God loves us? God's love surrounds us every day and will remain with us forever. Show the love of God to others today and accept the love He wants to show you.

Day 6

REMOVE THE STINGER

We shouldn't dwell on a hurt someone may have caused us. Dwelling on it just allows our hearts to get buried in it and blocks God from being able to do a work in us. We must allow God to drop the hurt. Having a forgiving heart is helping us to become more like God. Our prayer should be to live by the idea of "more of Him, less of me."

For if you forgive other people when they sin against you, your heavenly Father will also forgive you. But if you do not forgive others their sins, your Father will not forgive your sins. Matthew 6:14-15 (NIV)

We can't allow a hurt from someone else to build a wall between us and God. We weren't meant to understand everything, but God doesn't want us to. He wants us to believe that even the pain can be used to teach us and bring us closer to Him.

We must learn to show forgiveness in the ways God shows us. Not dwelling on the sting. When we get stung by a bee, it immediately starts to get red, swell, and become bothersome. It hurts! If the stinger stays in, it can become infected and cause even more pain.

We must remove our stinger so that we can heal. The longer we leave it in, the longer we allow our hearts to become bitter. The more bitter we get, the bigger the wall we build between us and God. It's okay to hurt from the sting, but don't allow it to become infected.

Journal

Day 7

Take time to meditate on God's word. What's on your heart this week?

_____

_____

_____

_____

_____

_____

_____

_____

_____

_____

_____

_____

_____

_____

_____

_____

_____

_____

_____

_____

Week Ten

Day 1

WHY ME?

"Why me?" Too often we get pulled so deep into the "why me" that we allow it to rule us. It becomes the reason we stop going to church, the reason we stop praying, or the reason we stop seeking God. It can even become the reason an addiction begins. We can become so entangled in the "why me" mentality that we start to believe that everyone and everything is against us, and nothing is for us. This is the furthest thing from the truth.

When you pass through waters, I will be with you; and when you pass through rivers, they will not sweep over you. When you walk through the fire, you will not be burned; the flames will not set ablaze.
Isaiah 43:2 (NIV)

God is always with us. We can choose to continue to play the victim role, or we can choose to have victory in Jesus.

But thanks be to God! He gives us the victory through our Lord Jesus Christ. 1 Corinthians 15:57 (NIV)

Day 2

HE NEVER STOPS

Have you ever started doubting God's power and love even though in the past you have seen His works in your life?

As they were talking about these things, Jesus himself stood among them, and said to them, "Peace to you!" But they were startled and frightened and thought they saw a spirit. And he said to them, "Why are you troubled, and why do doubts arise in your hearts? See my hands and my feet, that it is I myself. Touch me, and see. For a spirit does not have flesh and bones as you see that I have." And when he had said this, he showed them his hands and his feet. And while they still disbelieved for joy and were marveling, he said to them, "Have you anything here to eat?" They gave him a piece of broiled fish, and he took it and ate before them.
Luke 24:36-43

We've seen Him sustain and deliver, but then we fail to remember who He really is. In the scripture above, He says to His disciples, "Peace to you." When He says this, they are startled, frightened, and think they see a spirit. How many times does God offer us peace, and we turn it down for the flesh? We don't want His peace because we are seeking our own. We become startled and frightened by this because it's not what we want. We begin to replace the peace He's trying to give us with the peace we think we need.

And He said to them, "Why are you troubled, and why do doubts arise in your hearts? See my hands and my feet, that it is I myself. Touch me, and see. For a spirit does not have flesh and bones as you see that I have." And when He had said this, He showed them His hands and His feet. And while they still disbelieved for joy and were marveling...

We need to know that when we become troubled, and the doubts begin to rise, it may be because we are following the flesh instead of believing in God. We have seen and felt His works. We have been brought out of the darkness and delivered from evil, but when we become troubled, we still allow doubt to rise in our hearts. God still heals. As we allow ourselves to become dismayed and unraveled by our situations, God continues to show Himself to us.

...he said to them, "Have you anything here to eat?" They gave him a piece of broiled fish, and he took it and ate before them.

God will sometimes show Himself through scripture and through others, but no matter how He does it, He will never stop trying. Even when we continue to doubt, He will continue to attempt to get our attention. We don't serve a "give up" God. We serve a God that wants you to give in.

Day 3

FACED WITH OPPOSITION

Have you ever felt like you were imprisoned by a circumstance or by a situation? Have you ever felt like the weight of your problems was so heavy that you began to feel weighed down in defeat?

Today, we are going to go over three things you need to do when you are feeling that way.

In Acts, Peter was thrown into prison by Herod. He was chained down in between two soldiers when an angel appeared.

You may think an angel appearing in front of you seems far-fetched, but listening to God's direction, wisdom, and discernment is right at your doorstep through a relationship with Him. Peter was in tune with the Lord in His life.

And behold, an angel of the Lord stood next to him, and a light shone in the cell. He struck Peter on the side and woke him, saying, "Get up quickly." And the chains fell off his hands." Acts 12:7

This is something we should all do when facing opposition of any kind. We can stay down in our problems, or we can get up quickly giving no ground to the enemy. It's never too late to get up quickly!

*And the angel said to him, "Dress yourself and put on your sandals."
And he did so. And he said to him, "Wrap your cloak around you
and follow me." Acts 12:8
(A cloak symbolizes supernatural)*

What I love about this is that Peter is listening to the voice of God. The angel gives three demands; when we feel weighed down, these are also the three demands we need to follow:

1. Get up quickly
2. Dress yourself (put on the armor of God)
3. Wrap your cloak around you and follow me (put on His spirit and follow Him)

If you are facing something today or the next time opposition feels like it's chasing you down, remember these three steps.

God didn't intend for the chains to hold you down!

Day 4

LEADERS FOR CHRIST

Every year when my children go back to school and through each season of change, I am faced with new challenges, a few tears, and the task of learning to grow as a parent into who they need, not what they want. I am reminded that our God created us each individually for Him. As I think about what we should want to remind our children and even ourselves in these changing seasons, it's to be bold and to be different. We should stand out in a way that makes others want to have what we have inside of us, not what's seen on the outside. Our hearts should beam with God's light and shine so brightly that others want to follow it.

Don't let anyone look down on you because you are young, but set an example for the believers in speech, in conduct, in love, in faith, and in purity. 1 Timothy 4:12 (NIV)

Our children are our future leaders. We need to teach them that their value doesn't come from sports, grades, friends, or even us. They need to see that their true value only comes from God. When they realize that He values them more than anything in this world, they can begin to grow bold in their faith. They can become leaders by being examples to those around them.

They are leaders. We are leaders. They are strong, and they are beautiful because they were created with purpose in our Father's eyes.

Day 5

DON'T STAY STUCK

Have you ever felt stuck? Have you ever felt like you're sinking in quicksand, and you're not sure how you're going to get out? One thing gets stuck, then another, and before you know it, you have lost your freedom. You're stuck pretty badly, and no one's around to help.

"I will never leave you nor forsake you."
Hebrews 13:5

When hope's running low, and we feel all out of options, God says His options are endless, and His grace is overflowing.

God is always making a way (*Isaiah 43:19*) where we see no way.

God sees more than our eyes can see. He sees the bigger picture. When we think that we will be stuck forever, God tells us to quit relying on our ways and look to His. God could reach down, grab us, and just lift us out, but sometimes He wants to show us what He can do in the valleys to strengthen our faith and testimonies.

Being stuck isn't always bad. What you believe when you get stuck could be the difference between staying there or being freed.

Day 6

ONE OF A KIND

As I watched my little boy coloring one day, I thought to myself, "Man, that looks so good. He is staying in the lines and everything." That's what we are taught, and then what we teach to our kids. It's important to make sure we stay in all the lines when we color for it to look perfect and not messy.

You know, some of the most beautiful paintings are the ones that are abstract. The ones where the colors are overlapping and there are no lines. It's kind of like the people here on earth. Some of the most beautiful people have had some of the messiest lives.

He has made everything beautiful in its time.
Ecclesiastes 3:11

God can take anything and make it beautiful.

Sometimes we get lost in the fact that everything needs to be just right. We set boundaries on our lives when God has called us to trust and go outside of them for Him.

God can take any mess and do great wonders with it. In the middle of the process, we can't see the beauty that He sees. We can just see what we are handed at the time. We see the coloring sheet with a lot of mistakes. God sees the true masterpiece, the final product. All the colors come together, and He truly makes something that is one of a kind!

Journal

Day 7

Take time to meditate on God's word. What's on your heart this week?

_____

_____

_____

_____

_____

_____

_____

_____

_____

_____

_____

_____

_____

_____

_____

_____

_____

_____

_____

_____

Week Eleven

Day 1

QUICK TO LISTEN

My dear brothers and sisters, take note of this: Everyone should be quick to listen, slow to speak and slow to become angry.

James 1:19 (NIV)

We get so stuck on that "slow to speak and slow to become angry" part that a lot of times we can disregard one of the most beautiful things in this scripture, being "quick to listen."

I have to admit, I'm a better communicator than listener. I like to talk, I love to pour into others, and I can start a conversation with anyone. I tend to try and make those awkward situations just a little more comfortable, but I've realized that sometimes my ears are missing out on some of God's greatest blessings in my own life.

From a young age, our parents compete with each other about what the baby is going to say first. Is it going to be "dada" or "momma"? Then in school we have COM classes we can take to learn how to speak to people and address a crowd. There is absolutely nothing to teach us to be quiet.

God put it all into perspective for me. We cry out to Him, asking Him where He is. We pray and seek Him with words and sometimes feel like we aren't hearing anything from Him. We feel like He's disappeared, but it's because He's listening. How can He answer if we aren't finished with the plea? God's ears are open, and that's why He's always on time, why He always has the best answers, and why He never fails us.

Day 2

DENYING ONESELF FOR HIM

Have you ever read in John 18 when Peter denies Jesus? We can also tend to deny Him in many ways. We can deny doing what we know is right. We can deny the Holy Spirit when feeling convicted. We can deny the peace of God when giving in and not allowing His word to have more power than our own. We may not deny Jesus' name, but we can deny what He's trying to do in our hearts.

But in your hearts honor Christ the Lord as holy, always being prepared to make a defense to anyone who asks you for a reason for the hope that is in you; yet do it with gentleness and respect. 1 Peter 3:15

There is always a work that needs to be done through us for Him. Our hearts must always be open to accepting what God wants to give us. I will be the first to admit that it is not always easy, but I can also be the first to testify that it is always worth it. Pushing past the urge of handling things in the wrong way and allowing God to get the glory when we allow Him to handle them His way gives us peace. Following through with our convictions gives us the knowledge that His word holds more power than our own. Allowing His will to take precedence over ours can give us more peace and satisfaction. We sometimes deny what God is trying to do through us. What are you denying Him from working out within your heart today? When your heart feels pressured by the Holy Spirit to walk to the altar, are you still clinging to your seat? When you speak, are you speaking life or death? Don't keep Him from showing you what He has for you. Surrender yourself to Him and see what He can do in your life.

Day 3

DON'T LET IT HOLD YOU DOWN

We tend to dwell on our past and allow it to consume our now. God intended our past to help us grow and to build our future, but our past was never intended to weigh down the present. Nothing is too big for God, and no one is too far gone for God to move and show the grace He planted when He sent His Son to die on the cross.

For the grace of God has appeared, bringing salvation for all people.
Titus 2:11

God chose us all, not just some of us. He didn't choose us based on any criteria. God chose us all to save and show grace upon. No sin is too big for God to remove and then make us whole.

We can't allow our past to hold us back from what God has called of us now. The enemy wants to make us think that our past can have power over God's intentions for our future.

Don't let your past control your present. Grace was given on the cross to save us of all. Give God your past so that He can fulfill the plans He has for your today.

Day 4

BE STILL

A lot of times we go, go, go and forget something that's truly important in our walk with God.

Rest! God wants to give us rest when we are weary, but he also wants to give us rest when we are fine. He has even given us a day of rest, which is on the Sabbath day.

"Remember the Sabbath day, to keep it holy. Six days you shall labor, and do all your work, but the seventh day is a Sabbath to the Lord your God."
Exodus 20:8-10

Rest is not just meant for our bodies. Rest is meant for our souls and our minds. The Lord wants us to take time to rest in Him.

Whoever dwells in the shelter of the Most High will rest in the shadow of the Almighty. Psalm 91:1 (NIV)

The Lord offers a rest that can't be offered in the world, a rest from all things. He can give us a rest from the things that can make us burdened and tired: house duties, kids, money, bills, sicknesses, the list could go on and on. Our minds also seem to never stop thinking about trying to carry the load of everything.

The Lord wants us to let go of those thoughts and take shelter within Him.

He wants us to devote time to Him by reading, doing a devotion, praying, or just sitting in solitude with Him. God

wants to give you the rest you need in Him. Are you taking the time to rest, to really have that quiet time so He can speak to you through His word?

Don't forget that it's good to just "Be still".

Day 5

FIX YOUR EYES ON JESUS

We find joy in many things. Have you ever taken the time to think about where your joy comes from? Joy is a feeling of great pleasure and happiness. It's a "feel good." When I think of the word "joy," I think of a relationship with Christ. We will have true joy when we stop letting other things come before Him.

To me, joy stands for J-esus O-ver Y-ou.

Fixing our eyes on Jesus, the pioneer and perfecter of faith. For the joy set before him he endured the cross, scorning its shame, and sat down at the right hand of the throne of God. Hebrews 12:2 (NIV)

We get to rejoice knowing that we can fix our eyes on Jesus who has already endured our sorrow and misery on the cross.

We may get to experience a worldly happiness, but it's nothing in comparison to the true joy we can experience living for Jesus over ourselves. He brings a joy that is not prideful but is humbling. Think about those things that you believe bring you happiness, then replace them with Jesus. That's your joy. Joy is perfected through Him. We don't know joy the way we should until we put "J-esus O-ver Y-ou!"

Day 6

MAINTAINING GOOD HABITS

We all tend to run from something or someone (it could even be ourselves). Faith is depending on which direction you look. We can't accept things that don't belong to us. We must resist the negative that people bring or try to distribute on us. To resist these things, we have to maintain good habits. Habits revolved around God.

But in that coming day no weapon turned against you will succeed.
Isaiah 54:17 (NLT)

When we maintain good habits, we can arm ourselves. We can't change the world if we run from it. The more we are open to see what God can do, the more we see the amazing things that he proclaims over us. We must learn to walk in confidence. When we stop running from what we hate, we start realizing what we love. We need to have habits that contribute to our walk with God. What you may be running from could be the very thing that God is using to deliver you and to make you stronger in Him. Form habits for God that allow you to grow in grace.

Journal

Day 7

Take time to meditate on God's word. What's on your heart this week?

_____

_____

_____

_____

_____

_____

_____

_____

_____

_____

_____

_____

_____

_____

_____

_____

_____

_____

_____

_____

Week Twelve

Day 1

THE STING OF REJECTION

Most of us have felt the sting of rejection at some point in our lives. If you haven't felt it yet, it's inevitable that sometimes you will feel rejection, whether it's from loved ones, friends, a job, sports, or a simple forgotten invitation. We all go through it because we want to be accepted. Even Jesus felt rejection. In Mark 6 Jesus went to his hometown of Nazareth to teach, and the people who knew Him questioned Him and took offense at Him.

And Jesus said to them, "A prophet is not without honor, except in his hometown and among his relatives and in his own household."
Mark 6:4

A lot of times rejection comes from those closest to us, just as we reject the works God may be trying to do through us.

Just because we may be rejected by some, doesn't mean we can't make an impact on others. How many times have we rejected what Jesus has been trying to do through us or for us? How many times do we feel convicted but disregard it?

Jesus felt rejection just as we do; however, He didn't give up when the sting from the rejection of those closest to Him hit. Instead, even though he was rejected, the Bible says,

And he could do not mighty work there, except that he laid his hands on a few sick people and healed them. And he marveled because of their unbelief. And he went about among the villages teaching.
Mark 6:5-6

I think when we feel rejection, it's easy for us to feel the

need to give up. We need to realize that even if we aren't accepted by some, it doesn't mean we won't ever be accepted at all. Jesus' acceptance is what matters, and we need to remember that. Rejection can hurt, but it can also strengthen us. Don't carry the sting for too long. Remember, there are still others left to touch.

Day 2

DRINK THE LIVING WATER

When we drink from a water fountain, usually we are thirsty. We are needing to quench our thirst.

With God it's the same thing. We need to drink from God's fountain. We must satisfy ourselves with Him. When we are thirsty and fill ourselves from the wrong fountain (the world), we only partially satisfy ourselves until the well runs dry. We need to realize that we can't be fully satisfied without God.

God's well never runs dry, and He will always refresh you.

"For I will satisfy the weary soul, and every languishing soul I will replenish." Jeremiah 31:25

What well are you drinking from? If you feel empty, maybe you need to switch wells.

Day 3

PRAY IN CONFIDENCE

Do you believe in what you pray?

If you are anything like me, you tend to overanalyze things. When we overanalyze, we are allowing our own thoughts to outweigh Gods plans. We forget who and how big the God we serve is.

"Therefore I tell you, whatever you ask for in prayer, believe that you have received it, and it will be yours."
Mark 11:24

When we pray, God doesn't want us analyzing, He wants us believing. We must have faith in our prayers because we have faith in our God, who is bigger than our prayers.

God knows our needs. So, take the prayer that has not yet been answered, and pray for it in confidence today.

Be confident in the knowledge that the same God who loved us so much that He sent His Son to die for us is the same God who is answering our prayers. He's going to make sure they are answered just the way they are supposed to be.

No prayer is too big for God. Go to Him in confidence today.

Day 4

IT'S ALL IN THE APPROACH

Have you ever thought about the way we approach things and how it has an impact on the response we get? For instance, when we greet someone with a smile, more than likely we're going to get a smile from the other person in return. On the other hand, when we have a gloomy disposition, the other person will most likely ask us what's wrong or be grumpy in return.

How do we approach God?

The thing with God is that all He wants is our approach to be sincere and heartfelt. He wants us to come to Him happy, and He wants us to come sad. God doesn't care how we come as long as we come. He wants us to be real.

God knows our inner needs, desires, and feelings.

> *"Blessed are the pure in heart, for they shall see God."*
> *Matthew 5:8*

God wants your heart pure. He knows your heart, but He wants it to show what He already knows it to be.

Try approaching God today with a genuine heart.

Greet Him with your needs, and He will greet you with His riches.

Day 5

DON'T GET WRAPPED UP

The world takes so much out of us. Each week we are running around, working, paying bills, being there for others, cleaning, etc. We have a lot to do and a lot to keep up with. At times it becomes draining, overwhelming, and downright tiring. Sometimes we feel depleted and need a breath of fresh air. Well, I have good news for you.

When we feel attacked by the world, we can lean on God knowing that He only wants one thing from us.

He wants us to love Him!

My son, give me your heart, and let your eyes observe my ways.
Proverbs 23:26

Living life when we are only living it for worldly desires can be tough, but when we are living life only to love God, it's reassuring and a breath of fresh air.

Try not to go about your days so wrapped up in the "I gotta dos," and the "I needa haves.".

Delight in the fact that the world may seem like it needs so much from you, but God doesn't.

He just wants your love.

Day 6

GIVE IN

We have all heard the sayings, "Don't give up," "Keep going," "Keep pushing," "There is good coming," and "The breakthrough is on the other side." It's all good advice, but what if we changed it up a little, thought about it in a different way? What if we reworded it and instead of thinking of it as a "give up" we think of it as a "give in?"

"Just Give In"

So many times, in life we want to give up, but I think what God wants us to do is give in to what He has planned and to give up what we have planned. When we keep striving to make our own plans come to fruition, it gives Him no time to reveal His.

Too many of our plans for ourselves can become self-seeking or self-motivating, but when we hear the tiny whispers of God and wait for the plans, He has for us to unravel, it's far greater than anything we can even imagine putting together.

When we give in to His plans, His purpose will be revealed.

His plans come with purpose!

Many are the plans in a person's heart, but it is the Lord's purpose that prevails. Proverbs 19:21 (NIV)

Sometimes we may have to "give up" what we think we need so we can "give in" to what He wants us to receive! Let's "give in" to what God has for us today.

Journal

Day 7

Take time to meditate on God's word. What's on your heart this week?

_____

_____

_____

_____

_____

_____

_____

_____

_____

_____

_____

_____

_____

_____

_____

_____

_____

Week Thirteen

Day 1

BE READY FOR THE ATTACK

Temptation is not biased. We all fall short when it comes to temptation. The world knows how to reel us in and sometimes even hook us into doing things we shouldn't do or thinking things we shouldn't think. Temptation comes in many forms, and Satan knows all our weak points.

Satan even tried to tempt Jesus.

The Spirit immediately drove him out into the wilderness. And he was in the wilderness forty days, being tempted by Satan. And he was with the wild animals, and the angels were ministering to him.
Mark 1:12-13

Satan prowls on our weaknesses. What I love about this scripture is that, *"He was with the wild animals, and the angels were ministering to Him."* Knowing how strong He was, God still didn't let Jesus go out into the wilderness alone.

You aren't alone in your temptations either. There are others around you that can help you. I think we forget that doing life together with fellow Christians means "doing life" together. We aren't by ourselves. When you feel weakened by temptation, ask someone to pray with you, to claim scripture over you. Seek out what you need, and not what Satan is trying to pull you in with.

We know temptations will arise, but it's how we equip ourselves to fight them off that's important. Be ready for the attack, and know you aren't alone!

Day 2

PAY ATTENTION TO HIS WHISPERS

Has the Lord ever spoken to you in a whisper?

We are all hopeful that the Lord will come and speak to us when we are going through hard times, but I think sometimes God waits. It's not that He doesn't love us or want to help us. I think He waits because He wants our attention. To make sure we are listening.

And he said, "Go out and stand on the mount before the Lord." And behold, the Lord passed by, and a great and strong wind tore the mountains and broke in pieces the rocks before the Lord, but the Lord was not in the wind. And after the wind an earthquake, but the Lord was not in the earthquake. And after the earthquake a fire, but the Lord was not in the fire. And after the fire the sound of a low whisper. 1 Kings 19:11-12

We strive to figure out what God is trying to tell us in our battles, but sometimes the understanding can't come until the storm gets quiet. We pray for guidance throughout the storm, but when the storm has passed may be when our attention is completely on Him, and we will be able to hear His tiny whispers.

Day 3

PUT ON LOVE

We wake up in the morning, get out of bed, and try to decide what we are going to wear. If we're really smart, we've already picked it out the night before. (That's not me though, so don't feel bad if you don't either.) We get dressed and go about our day. This got me to thinking, as we get up and get ready for the day, it would also be a good idea to get up and get ready for God.

And above all of these put on love, which binds everything together in perfect harmony. Colossians 3:14

Do you put on anything for God in the morning?

It's true, we wake up and face the day with the attitude and outlook we choose. Are you waking up and clothing yourself in love?

Wearing love is wearing God.

When we put on love, we decide to live as God lives for us. Love brings all things together.

This morning put on love before you walk out the door. Let's see how clothing yourself in love makes a difference in your day!

Day 4

CLOSE TO THE BROKEN-HEARTED

No one is exempt from dealing with the pain and heartache that death brings. God sends others who may have been through similar experiences to encourage us and to lift us up so that we have someone to walk beside us, but there is nothing like the love of God during tough times.

No one can truly understand your pain like He does.
No one can comprehend your heart like He does.
No one can heal like He does.

The best advice is to turn to His word. Scripture states that He is always with the broken-hearted.

> *"He heals the brokenhearted and binds up their wounds."*
> *Psalm 147:3*

God had to deal with the death of His son. He wasn't exempt from one of the most painful events we must face as humans. More importantly, He deals with the death of His children daily from losing them to this world.

> *My flesh and my heart may fail, but God is the strength of my heart and my portion forever. Psalm 73:26*

We aren't supposed to bear the weight of death. We are not always meant to comprehend everything. Our God needs to be our comprehension in those times. He must be our embrace. No one can embrace you in the midst of pain like He can. When we as humans don't have the right things to

say, He knows exactly what to do. From wiping our tears to cushioning our fall. He will mend our hearts if we seek His understanding through it all.

"Blessed are those who mourn, for they will be comforted."
Matthew 5:4

Day 5

SERVE HIM FIRST

Don't we all like to feel wanted, to be liked, and to have the approval of others?

We don't feel accepted when we feel neglected.

We tend to focus on worldly approval far more than we focus on the approval of God. We become people pleasers and we become miserable. Do you know how hard it is to please everyone or to feel the need to? The greatest thing is that the One whom we should seek approval from and aim to please will always accept us. He loves us with the good, the bad, and the ugly.

For am I now seeking the approval of man, or of God? Or am I trying to please man? If I were still trying to please man, I would not be a servant of Christ.
Galatians 1:10

We can't be a servant of both man and Christ. When we are trying to be a servant to both, we aren't giving our all to the One that matters.

I've spent so much of my life wanting the acceptance of others and hoping that in return I had their approval. Once I realized that I had already been accepted by the One who mattered most, I started living a life pleasing to God because I knew that His approval was all that mattered.

We are His servants above all else.

Day 6

CONFIDENCE COMES FROM THE HEART

What does confidence in Christ look like?

We have confidence in a lot of things, from people to our own abilities. Confidence can be put in tangible and intangible things. Confidence is feeling certain about the truth of something.

Let us with confidence draw near to the throne of grace, that we may receive mercy and find grace to help in the time of need. Hebrews 4:16

Confidence in Christ is the highest level of faith. It's knowing who we are in Him on the outside and on the inside. Confidence is knowing God has moved in our lives, and that He can move again. It is seeing God's way when our road seems closed. Confidence is when our legs feel weak from running so long, but we know that the finish line is right ahead. Confidence is knowing that God has carried, still carries, and will continue to carry us. Our true confidence is found in Christ. We may feel confident in ourselves, in our abilities, and in our outward appearance, but confidence is reflected from our hearts. When our hearts reflect confidence, they reflect Jesus Christ.

Let's grow in confidence towards God.

For we are the circumcision, who worship by the spirit of God and glory in Christ Jesus and put no confidence in flesh. Philippians 3:3

Journal

Day 7

Take time to meditate on God's word. What's on your heart this week?

_____

_____

_____

_____

_____

_____

_____

_____

_____

_____

_____

_____

_____

_____

_____

_____

_____

_____

_____

Week Fourteen

Day 1

LET IT GO

Words cut deep, and actions can hurt to the core, but it's still important for us to forgive. I've always heard the saying hurt people hurt people. Everyone experiences feelings differently, and sometimes emotions can run high. What's important, though, is that when we've been wronged, we always offer the gift of forgiveness.

Holding onto bitter feelings only makes us bitter people. Forgiveness shows God's grace. When God resides in us, so does a heart of forgiveness. The longer we allow ourselves to harbor negative feelings, the longer the enemy has to work on his plan. When we hold onto bitterness and unforgiveness, we allow the enemy to have control over our minds and take precedence over what's in our hearts.

Put on then, as God's chosen ones, holy and beloved, compassionate hearts, kindness, humility, meekness, and patience, bearing with one another and, if one has a complaint against another, forgiving each other; as the Lord has forgiven you, so you also must forgive.
Colossians 3:12-13

As a child of God, we are to offer what He gave and still gives. Forgiveness comes from the heart where He resides. Don't give the enemy power in your life. Allow yourself to be released from the hurt. It's time to offer the forgiveness that God offers us. It's time to let it go!

Day 2

FEAR DOESN'T CHANGE THE OUTCOME

Picture yourself in a dark room with a tank. You are supposed to reach your hand down in it and figure out what's in there. It could be a soft teddy bear, or it could be a snake. Most likely, you aren't going to just reach your hand in without being extremely fearful of the outcome. A lot of people treat life the same way. They don't want to trust God with their families, their homes, or even the situations they are in because they are fearful of the unknown. What's going to be the outcome if they give it all to God?

It reminded me of the story in the Bible when the Lord wanted Moses to bring the Israelites out of Egypt.

Then Moses answered, "But behold, they will not believe me or listen to my voice, for they will say, 'The Lord did not appear to you.'" The Lord said to him, "What is that in your hand?" He said, "A staff." And he said, "Throw it on the ground." So he threw it on the ground, and it became a serpent, and Moses ran from it.
Exodus 4:1-3

God continued in the next verses to show Moses who He was. He had him catch the snake by the tail, and the snake became the staff again. He continued to give Moses signs to prove who He was and to show that what He had planned for Moses was good.

We can all be fearful of the unknown, but I want to tell you that being afraid will not change the outcome. God knows

the outcomes, and the plans that He has for us are to prosper us. Whether we fear the plans He has for us or the unknown will not change anything. God doesn't want us to be afraid of what He knows will be good and mighty for our lives. Whatever you are fearing, you must remember God's hand is on it. Allow your fear to be replaced with trust. When you have God, you have a director. Don't allow yourself to become fearful of the unknown. When God is that unknown, there is nothing to fear.

Day 3

GOD-SIZED STRENGTH

No matter how in shape we are, our body-fat ratios, or the size of our muscles, strength comes from within us. Strength can only come from the Lord. We may have the title "The Strongest Man" or "The Strongest Woman," but if God doesn't live inside of us, our strength is only physical.

That strength will fade, but the Lord's will remain the same.

Think about the story of David and Goliath. David was fighting someone way bigger than he was, but with his God-sized strength and God-sized faith, he won. What size is your strength today? A God-sized strength? A God-sized strength can lift any weight. God-sized strength is knowing that He's already lifted the weight.

"The Lord is my strength and my song, and he has become my salvation; this is my God, and I will praise him, my father's God, and I will exalt him. The Lord is a man of war; the Lord is his name."
Exodus 15:2-3

Day 4

COME TOGETHER

People sometimes question why God would allow bad things to happen to innocent people, but people allow these things to happen to innocent people. We have a choice. They have a choice. God loves us so much that He allows us to decide whether we will follow Him or whether we will allow the enemy to have power through us in this world. We as believers need to realize just how big the enemy is.

"The thief comes only to steal and kill and destroy."
John 10:10

The enemy comes to kill our dreams, ambitions, and hope. The enemy then starts to steal our hearts and minds and destroy our homes. He doesn't stop there. He begins to destroy who we are and makes us believe his lies. "You aren't good enough." "You'll never live up to that." "You're a failure and a misfit, and you can't do anything right." Once you give him that power, he moves on to breaking you down in other areas. He's real, and when we give him power, he can start to take over our feelings and our lives.

"I came so that they may have life and have it abundantly."
John 10:10

The enemy is big, but God is MUCH BIGGER! We, as Christians, have a responsibility to reach others. If the enemy can break down, God can build up, and we have to reach out! Just as God lives within us, the enemy finds those he can live within. Sin can stand out, but Jesus already stood in! He gave us this world to reach those souls. If

Jesus stood in for us we must stand in for others. Grace, mercy, and hope are all things God offers to this world. He offers a life far greater than death. We must come together. Others need to encounter God!

Day 5

UNRAVEL THE WHY

We are faced with times in our lives when we just don't understand. In those times, we ask God for understanding, for hope, and for a reason why we are having to go through them. I don't always like to ask why because I want my faith to be bigger than that, but sometimes I think asking why is a way of humbling yourself before God and showing that you need Him. The "why" can be the transition into God's answer.

Trust in the Lord with all your heart, and do not lean on your own understanding. In all of your ways acknowledge him, and he will make straight your paths.
Proverbs 3:5-6

I think trust is key. When we don't understand, we have to trust that God has a plan. When we need reasons, we must trust that God has His motivations. Sometimes understanding really means to just trust in the process.

If God knits us together in our mother's wombs and loves us enough to wipe away our sins, I think we can put our trust in Him. When we don't understand our season and the walls feel like they are falling, we must remember that He is our hope. When we trust in His process, He will eventually shed light upon it for our own understanding.

Let God unravel your why and reveal what you may not understand.

Day 6

THE BUILD UP

"If you faint in the day of adversity, your strength is small."
Proverbs 24:10

Very rarely do you just roll out of bed and want to have a bad day. You are hopeful it's going to go smoothly. Your kids will listen, and work will be a blessing. Then it happens, you step on some legos your kids have left out, your husband has misplaced your keys, and it looks as if someone has fast forwarded the clock because you have become 15 minutes late. Oh, that's not the end of it. When will someone ever figure out that little thing called traffic?

It's not just a small thing that happens that sets our mood for the day, it's usually the buildup that gets us there. I'm guilty for allowing the buildup to dictate the rest of my day. What we have, though, is the freedom to decide not to allow that to happen. We can stop the buildup and build our relationships with God.

We tend to keep going and allow ourselves to keep getting frustrated because we don't stop and give God a minute of our time. In the buildup, God may be trying to show us or teach us something. Why don't we take a minute to listen?

Stop. Don't allow yourself to build a wall of frustration, anger, and hurt between you and God. Tear the wall down before it's even built. Take a second, say a prayer, and ask for help. That wall can be knocked down by the presence of the Lord faster than it can be put up.

Journal

Day 7

Take time to meditate on God's word. What's on your heart this week?

_____

_____

_____

_____

_____

_____

_____

_____

_____

_____

_____

_____

_____

_____

_____

_____

_____

_____

_____

_____

Week Fifteen

Day 1

A FIRM FOUNDATION

The foundation of a house is what's supposed to be the strongest part of a house; what everything else is built upon. If it didn't have the foundation, the rest of the house wouldn't be sturdy. It would lack the support it needed.

When we think of our family, we need to think of them as the house and God as our foundation. Our "house" needs to be firmly built on God.

> *"Everyone then who hears these words of mine and does them will be like a wise man who built his house on the rock. And the rain fell, and the floods came, and the winds blew and beat on that house, but it did not fall, because it had been founded on the rock. And everyone who hears these words of mine and does not do them will be like a foolish man who built his house on the sand. And the rain fell, and the floods came, and the winds blew and beat against that house, and it fell, and great was the fall of it."*
> *Matthew 7:24-27*

God is our rock. He is our foundation. When we build our families on God's word, we can withstand all attacks from the enemy. When the trials and tribulations come, and the strong winds blow, our homes will not be shaken because our foundations have been built on "The Rock".

Let's make sure our homes are built on God so we can withstand the rain and the storms.

Day 2

LOVE YOURSELF

Before we can ever love others the way God desires, we must be able to love God first. Once we love God the way we were meant to, then we must learn to love ourselves the way He has intended. Then after we have figured out those two loves, we can love others with an intentional love.

When we love someone, we are devoted to them. We are gentle, kind, honest, impassioned, and patient. We spend time with those we love. We call them, visit them, and even pray over them. God should be at the top of the list of our loves. We need to be actively doing the same things and more with Him. God doesn't need our love, but He longs for our love. If we have time to love on people, we have to make time to love on God.

"'And you shall love the Lord your God with all your heart and with all your soul and with all your mind and with all your strength.' The second is this: 'You shall love your neighbor as yourself.' There is no other commandment greater than these." Mark 12:30-31

First, we are to love God with our whole being. Then it says, "Love your neighbor as yourself." If we don't love ourselves, we can't love our neighbor the way we are supposed to. Loving ourselves means meditating on the word, respecting our bodies, getting the sleep we need, and fueling ourselves with what we need and not what we want.

Here we find the order of love: God, ourselves, and then we will be able to give the right kind of love to those around us.

Day 3

FRIENDS GIVE GRACE

Have you ever had a friend make you mad or upset, and you decided that, today, instead of showing them the grace they deserve you, were going to ignore them? Or even worse, you totally didn't agree with what they did or posted so you condemned them for it and ran and talked to another friend about it? Now, we all can show a little transparency and say we've done this before.

A friend loves at all times, and a brother is born to adversity.
Proverbs 17:17

A faithful friend loves despite differences; despite whether they agree with what we are doing or going through. A faithful friend shows love always. We don't pick and choose when we love or what we are going to love them through. We decide we are going to love them despite the adversity in their life. Friends give grace.

Prayer: Lord help us all to be better friends. Friends that love no matter the circumstance. Friends that show grace and aren't quick to run to others. Lord help us to be the friend to others that you are to us. Amen

Day 4

BUBBLE OF COMFORT

Who truly likes to be uncomfortable? I think we all like to live in comfort. Do you know that God didn't call us to be comfortable? Sometimes it takes us getting a little uncomfortable to go where God is calling us. If everything were comfortable, then we would always stay in our own bubble. We would never extend ourselves into God's level of discomfort.

Let me give you an example. It truly made me uncomfortable to publish this devotional book. I knew that once I put all my writings out there, it would make me vulnerable to criticism. That scared me and made me super uncomfortable. I don't like conflict, and I don't deal with criticism very well. Usually it is followed by awkward silence or going to a secluded place and staying there for a while.

If I didn't publish this book despite my discomfort, I wouldn't be truly serving God with my talents to my full ability. God has given me words and a voice to use. I realized I needed to step out of my bubble and make myself uncomfortable so that God could use me the way He intended to.

Are you limiting your talents to a bubble? If so, let yourself get a little uncomfortable, and see the comfort God brings to you.

"You did not choose me, but I chose you and appointed you that you should go and bear fruit and that your fruit should abide, so that whatever you ask the Father in my name, he may give it to you." John 15:16

Day 5

RID YOURSELF OF BITTERNESS

Those around us can be bitter and angry. That, in return, can start to dictate our own moods. From evil looks or rude comments from a co-worker to the road rage that can happen on the way to work, little things throughout the day can bring us down. Everything has a part to play in our day and in our moods.

Get rid of all bitterness, rage, anger, harsh words, and slander, as well as all types of evil behavior. Instead, be kind to each other, tenderhearted, forgiving one another, just as God through Christ has forgiven you.
Ephesians 4:31-32 (NLT)

Even when others don't show love and compassion, it's our job to show them what God has shown us. When we do wrong, God forgives us. We, in return, must forgive them. It made me think of the verse,

Jesus said, "Father, forgive them, for they don't know what they are doing." Luke 23:34 (NLT)

Think about all the times we've not known what we were doing, and God still chose to forgive us. Everyone's walk is different, and we have to pray that they'll learn something from the love and compassion that is projected through us. God wants us all to be better people, kinder people, and more forgiving people. Lord, allow us to walk away from ill will and remember to continuously show love to others!

Day 6

CLEANSE OUR HEARTS

How well does God know us? Well, He knows every inch of our being. How well do we know ourselves, though? Sometimes we struggle with that. We must go through experiences that mold and shape us.

Search me, O God, and know my heart! Try me and know my thoughts! Psalm 139:23-24

This would be a great prayer. A tough prayer, but great. We want God to search us and cleanse our lives of our sins. We want our hearts to be purified. When God is searching us, there may be dirty things that come to the surface; past wounds that continue to keep us from our callings. God knows our hearts, and he can cleanse and make us whole again. We need to ask him to try us, to make us pure in our thoughts and help us to become gracious in our actions. If there are any grievous ways in us, we should ask Him to cleanse them from our thoughts and lead us to His steadfast love.

Prayer: God I ask that you make us new today and every day. Lord keep our thoughts directed on you and cleanse our hearts from any impurities.

Journal

Day 7

Take time to meditate on God's word. What's on your heart this week?

_____

_____

_____

_____

_____

_____

_____

_____

_____

_____

_____

_____

_____

_____

_____

_____

_____

_____

_____

_____

Week Sixteen

Day 1

WHERE'S YOUR TREASURE?

What do you treasure? Some may say their kids, spouse, a friendship, possessions, or even their abilities. Everyone has something that comes to mind when they think of something they treasure. Something they value.

"For where your treasure is, there your heart will be also."
Matthew 6:21

We all know that where we put our time and effort is where we will be rewarded. Well, when we put our earthly treasures over our greatest treasure, our reward is light. The biggest pot of gold we've been given wasn't placed at the end of a rainbow, it was nailed to a cross.

The treasure that comes with our biggest reward is gained in and through our salvation. Accepting Jesus Christ is the biggest gift anyone could ever obtain. When we see Jesus Christ as our gift from God, we don't just have a treasure; we can begin to believe we are treasured. Our hearts are full, not on worldly gain, but on heavenly fulfillment.

Our treasure was beaten and bruised
Our treasure was nailed to a cross
Our treasure rose from the dead
Our treasure brought us new life
Our hearts only contain true treasure
when it contains Jesus Christ.

Do you find your treasure in Jesus? Where is your heart today? Let it be in the greatest treasure ever to be found. The one who paid the biggest price.

Day 2

CHECK YOUR TENT

Are we open to what God is trying to say to us? I think about how aggravating it is when my kids don't listen to me. It also frustrates me for them because I know there are consequences to not listening, like having to learn the hard way. God probably thinks the same of us when He continues to try to teach us, but we continue to not listen. Thank goodness, though, that His love is so unconditional that even when we choose to not listen, He never gives up on us.

To paraphrase Genesis 13, Abram, later renamed by God Abraham, and Lot separated because there wasn't enough land to support them both. Abram stayed obedient to God and pitched his tent by the oaks of Mamre, but Lot chose to pitch his tent in Sodom. Sodom was a place where there was great wickedness and many sinners.

This reminded me that we must be careful where we pitch our tents. God blesses obedience, as he does for Abram later in the story, but I believe we truly have a still, small voice that speaks to us when we choose to listen. Lot put himself in a wicked place with sinners which in return made others question his faith. God, however, rescues us from those places and times we choose not to listen. He does the same for Lot.

"Call to me and I will answer you, and tell you great and hidden things that you have not known."
Jeremiah 33:3

We need to be obedient to where God is calling us and

make sure we aren't pitching our tents in the wrong places or with the wrong people. We should be mindful of what God puts on our hearts and careful to listen to what He speaks to us. I think we all need to make sure we are evaluating where our tents are pitched and make sure they don't need to be moved.

Day 3

BUT HE CAN

Have you ever felt like there was a war raging around you? The enemy continues to attack us in our minds; with sickness and with turmoil. It just seems like there are seas brewing, and we can't foresee the calmness after the storm. Sometimes we feel like we have the odds stacked against us, and it's hard not to fear. We start to allow the enemy to gain access to our minds, and instead of stopping him before he gains power, our fear becomes bigger than our faith.

Though an army encamp against me, my heart shall not fear; though war arise against me, yet I will be confident.
Psalm 27:3

We are nothing without Him. We can't walk through raging waters, but HE CAN.

We can't fight against an army of anxious thoughts, but HE CAN.

We can't heal our bodies and our souls, but HE CAN.

When the war seems to be intense, we must remember we may not be able to win it, but HE CAN!

There is peace in just knowing HE CAN and HE WILL!

Day 4

GIVE YOURSELF HIS DAILY BREAD

What good is it if we say something but do something different? What good do we do if we try to teach our children one thing, but we don't practice the same? We wouldn't go to school to be an engineer and then go in practice as a doctor.

What good is it, my brothers, if someone says he has faith but does not have works? Can that faith save him? If a brother or sister is poorly clothed and lacking in daily food, and one of you says to them, "Go in peace, be warmed and filled," without giving them the things needed for the body, what good is that? So also faith by itself, if it does not have works, is dead. James 2:14-17

What good is our faith if we don't seek Him out? What good can we do if we aren't putting the good inside of us? We need Him for our bodies, our minds, and for His spirit to grow within us. If we aren't being filled with what we need to keep our faith alive, then our faith can become dead.

Can we give to others if our faith is dead?

It's so important that we keep our faith alive for us to stay alive. We know that we must eat, drink, and take care of ourselves. We must feed ourselves the word, drink from His well, and love ourselves the way we are supposed to.

Let Him be your daily food today.

Day 5

WALK WITH ME

*Then Job answered and said: "Today also my complaint is bitter; my
hand is heavy on account of my groaning."*
Job 23:1-2

How many times in our own life do we question God as to
where He is? When we don't hear from Him and things are
unraveling around us, we begin to think He has left us. We
fail to see that it's maybe we who have left Him. God
NEVER goes anywhere.

What happens if our trust is lost, our faith is weakened, our
fear becomes prominent, and it seems that God has left us?

"He will never leave you or forsake you."
Deuteronomy 31:6

I think that when we start to question where God is, we
need to turn it around and say, "Where are we?" Aren't we
seated in the palm of His hands? Does He not have our
hand in His? God never goes anywhere. He is with us
every step of the way. During those times when He seems
far away, it's our job to pull in closer. More than likely we
have allowed our fleshly misconceptions to push us farther.

*"Where were you when I laid the foundation of the earth? Tell me, if
you have understanding. Who determined its measurements-surely you
know! Or who stretched the line upon it?" Job 38:4-5*

*"Shall a faultfinder contend with the almighty? He who argues with
God, let him answer it." Job 40:2*

This silenced Job. The word of the Lord is powerful. Who are we to question God? Truly, God has all the answers. We can't even comprehend some of those answers or the reasoning behind them, but surely, if He knows where to mark off the land from the sea and how to create us so perfectly in our mother's womb, we should trust Him.

Instead of asking God where He is, say to God, "Where am I? Walk me through this path I'm on and don't allow me to get lost in it. Be with me exactly where I am. Let me find your purpose and plan in this very moment."

Day 6

NEW ALWAYS WEARS OFF

Some of us spend our whole lives chasing after things that will give us nothing. We find a little fleeting happiness in those things but never gain what we truly need from them. Some chase money, some chase possessions, and some chase thrills. We continue to replace each chase with a new one hoping the next will make us happier than the one before, but when the next thing also offers only momentary happiness, we are stuck looking for something new again.

New always wears off!

One thing that never will get old, will never wear off, and is always new is God's love for us.

I love those who love me, and those who seek me diligently find me.
Proverbs 8:17

Why not chase after the one thing that can remain constant in your life? God can supersede any money, possession, or thrill. When we stop looking to chase worldly things and focus on the one right thing, we then experience the joy of feeling real happiness.

I'm here to tell you we cannot find real happiness within ourselves nor with anything other than God. Everything else is secondary compared to what He has to offer. Our spouses and even our kids cannot bring us true joy until our heart is completely set on chasing the Lord. Stop chasing after the wrong things. Chase after the one and only thing that is true light. He's waiting for you.

Journal

Day 7

Take time to meditate on God's word. What's on your heart this week?

_____

_____

_____

_____

_____

_____

_____

_____

_____

_____

_____

_____

_____

_____

_____

_____

_____

_____

_____

Week Seventeen

Day 1

NO GIFT IS TOO SMALL

We have all been called to serve God. None of us lead the same lives, nor do we have the exact same calling. God uses us all for different purposes and with different plans already constructed.

Only let each person lead the life that the Lord has assigned to him, and to which God has called him. This is my rule in all the churches.
1 Corinthians 7:17

What's your gift?
Do you have a gift of praying? Then pray for others.
Do you have a gift of singing? Then praise.
Do you have a gift of making others smile? Then reach out to the wounded and broken hearted.
Do you have a gift of organization? Then start planning.

No gift is too small for God to use. God has crafted each of us with important talents, some of which change throughout our lives. He wants us to use those gifts to reach others in our paths. By reaching out a hand to pray, reaching up a hand to praise, or bringing laughter to your surroundings, you have no idea who you can touch.

God uses us just as we are to bring others to Him just as they are.

For we are his workmanship, created in Christ Jesus for good works, which God prepared beforehand, that we should walk in them.
Ephesians 2:10

All of our gifts and talents were handcrafted by our Father exclusively for you and me. God knew exactly how He could use us. Don't let what's been handcrafted for you go to waste. He can use anything, from the smallest to the greatest, to touch the world. Use what your Father gave you and use it for His good!

Day 2

THE IMAGE HE SEES

How many times have we looked in the mirror and wished we could change something? I no longer want to look in the mirror and see myself. I want to look in the mirror and see God.

We shouldn't want to see change on the outside, but we should want to see the change He has done internally. We should no longer find fault in a false image of ourselves; we should find the perfection He has created inside of us.

We shouldn't want to blend in. We should want to stand out. We should want such a bright light to shine from inside of us that when we look at ourselves in the same mirror in which we used to see our imperfections, we now see the exact image He sees. We shouldn't view ourselves through the world's shallow eyes. We need to see ourselves through His eyes. We need to see the "me" He created, not the "me" the world may perceive.

You are altogether beautiful, my love; there is no flaw in you.
Song of Solomon 4:7

Let's stop viewing ourselves negatively. What He sees when He looks at us is a unique creation. We are always our own worst critics. Can you imagine how He feels when we put ourselves under a microscope and tear ourselves down? We are criticizing His own creation! We need to want Him so deeply rooted within us that His light shines to the outside. We need His beauty to be in that mirror. When I look in the mirror, I want to see me fully engulfed by Him. Let's see the "me" He made!

Day 3

TAKE YOUR TRASH OUT

One of my biggest pet peeves is a trash can that's overflowing. A dirty trash bin can make the whole house smell. Our lives can be much like a dirty trash can. We allow ourselves to become overwhelmed when we don't take the time to take out the trash that is consuming our lives. The trash that we're keeping around can then begin to show on the outside.

When we accept Jesus as our Savior, He cleanses us from our sins, but what we allow in from that point can be considered trash to our souls.

Cleanse me with hyssop, and I will be clean; wash me, and I will be whiter than snow. Psalm 51:7 (NIV)

In this verse David is wanting a spiritual cleansing. Sometimes, just as we bathe to get clean on the outside, we also need to bathe the inside by taking the trash out and asking God for a spiritual cleansing of our souls. We can allow "trash" to enter our lives by our actions, things we watch on television, from others, or even in secret sins. When you know your trash can may be getting full, it's important to ask God to help you get spiritually cleansed before it overflows.

We all need to take time to take the trash out!

Day 4

ENCOURAGE OTHERS

Two is always better than one. As God's children, we are here to spread love and to encourage one another. I know that without some of my closest friends I would have had a much more difficult time stepping out in faith to start a women's ministry. It took a few driven women and a lot of dedication. I would lie if I didn't say I was fearful of what others would think or say. I was worried about who would or would not come. I feared the judgement that would come from putting myself out there, but I had others pushing me and building me up. I had supportive women working with me and not tearing me down. We are supposed to stir each other to do acts for Jesus.

And let us consider how to stir up one another to love and good works, not neglecting to meet together, as is the habit of some, but encouraging one another, and all the more as you see the Day drawing near.
Hebrews 10:24-25

We all need reassurance, support, and motivation. It's easy to forget to lift up others when we may need the uplifting ourselves. The God we serve is our main encouragement! We can be encouraged to know that we serve a God that will never leave us. We may be that exact thing God is using to help encourage someone else today.

Today I challenge you to be a light of encouragement to someone. There is great power in encouragement. God can use us to show His love to those we meet. I challenge you to step out of your comfort zone and have faith that with God as our encouragement we are capable of all things. See how far a little encouragement can go today.

Day 5

DRINK FROM HIS WELL

When peace flows through our veins and lives in our hearts it surely directs our way. We all battle with feelings of worry, doubt, anxiety, and fear. Our inner battle with these things takes away the peace God means for us to have. God wants to give us a peace within our souls that overpowers our fears. It's natural to feel the weight of worry, the weight of doubt, and the weight of fear, but God doesn't want that weight to determine what's in our souls. He wants it to be "WELL" in our soul.

And the peace of God, which surpasses all understanding, will guard your hearts and your mind in Christ Jesus.
Philippians 4:7

Our God gives us what we need to say it is well when He is the well, we are drinking from. When we are being fueled by the word, we live from a spirit-filled well. Even all the doubt, fear, and worry can be transformed into a peace that surpasses all understanding. God's well was meant to be how we fuel our own souls. When we drink from His well, it will always be well in our soul!

Day 6

GIVE YOURSELF FULLY TO HIM

And as he was setting out on his journey, a man ran up and knelt before him and asked him, "Good Teacher, what must I do to inherit eternal life?" And Jesus said to him, "Why do you call me good? No one is good except God alone. You know the commandments: 'Do not murder, Do not commit adultery, Do not steal, Do not bear false witness, Do not defraud, Honor your father and mother.'" And he said to him, "Teacher, all these I have kept from my youth." And Jesus, looking at him, loved him, and said to him, "You lack one thing: go, sell all that you have and give to the poor, and you will have treasure in heaven; and come, follow me." Disheartened by the saying, he went away sorrowful, for he had great possessions.
Mark 10:17-22

These are some eye-opening scriptures. This man is coming to Jesus wanting to know how to be saved; how he could have eternal life in heaven. In this scripture, Jesus tells him no one is good except God alone. It shows how humble Jesus was and how we should also humble ourselves. It also teaches us that judgement cannot come from anyone but God. We are all sinners, and we all live in a broken world.

We can all relate to this man. God constantly shows us how much He loves us, and we continue to choose other things over Him. There are things we are afraid to give up. We want the treasure, but we aren't willing to sacrifice what we have for it. Our things are more important to us than completely trusting and loving Jesus Christ.

It may not be possessions for you, but it may be a sin, like condemning others. You may be putting others or something else above God, but Jesus tells us that we will

receive great treasure in heaven when we turn over our sins to him and choose to follow him. Don't walk away from what God has for you out of fear of giving up something in your life. It is nothing compared to the treasure you will receive in heaven. Give your life fully to Jesus.

Journal

Day 7

Take time to meditate on God's word. What's on your heart this week?

_____

_____

_____

_____

_____

_____

_____

_____

_____

_____

_____

_____

_____

_____

_____

_____

_____

_____

_____

Week Eighteen

Day 1

HE IS FOR ME

Do you ever remind yourself in the stillness that God is God and He is always good? We must remind ourselves in the very quiet and in the very busy times in life that there is no one like Him. When we are searching for answers and hoping for change, we need to remind ourselves that He has never left us and He will not forsake us. There is no one else that will be for us like He is.

We have to always remember that true happiness cannot and will not come from anything other than the one true Lord! I am thankful today and every day that I am who I am through Christ Jesus who saved me! Below is something I wrote from the love I have for Him. It's good in the stillness and the busy times to just stop and praise Him.

"For Me"

When there may be others against me, You will always stand in for me. When my hope is drowned out by things I cannot change, You will change them for me. When I lose strength and become weak, You will always fight for me.

If God is for us, who can be against us?
Romans 8:31

Our feet should be planted on His word and not on others' descriptions of who we are. Our feet should planted on four words that stand firm forevermore, "He is for me." That's all that matters. When we have Him in our hearts, no one can take that away. You are His and He is yours!

Day 2

RAP SHEET

Love is patient, love is kind. It does not envy, it does not boast, it is not proud. It does not dishonor others, it is not self-seeking, it is not easily angered, it keeps no record of wrongs.
1 Corinthians 13:4-5 (NIV)

Whose rap sheet are you trying to create? We all do it. In your mind are you keeping a list of things you don't agree with...things they did, said, or are doing? Have you ever thought those things may be some of your very own convictions? You can't love the way God has intended you to if you're writing rap sheets with someone else's name at the top of them.

Love keeps no record of wrongs. If you're recording someone else's faults, mistakes, or imperfections in a list in your head, your name could only be God. However, our God doesn't even do that. Everything we have done isn't on a rap sheet, it is voided and forgiven. We shouldn't have anyone else's rap sheet memorized to repeat to ourselves or even to others. If you're harboring hurt in your heart, then you're imprisoned in resentment.

The only sheet I want my name on is a page in "The Book Of Life," and that is written down the day you give your life to Jesus Christ. God doesn't even keep up with a rap sheet, so neither should we!

Day 3

OPEN ARMS

God wants us to come to Him, not expecting anything, but ready to receive something.

Too many times, we go to God in want of something but don't realize that our want may not be our need. Instead of Him doing what we expect, He could be preparing us for what we need to receive.

God is unfaltering. When we are weak, we depend on Him. God wants us to come to Him, not being closed to everything except what we want, but being open to what He can give!

May God our Father and the Lord Jesus Christ give you grace and peace. 2 Thessalonians 1:2 (NLT)

God's the giver of all, and even though we may not always know what we truly need, we must remember that God's love for us is deeper than we realize. He always knows the desires of our hearts, but He also knows what we have been called for. We forget that some things may be essential for our growth.

Go to Him with open arms, ready to receive what He has prepared for you.

Day 4

STAY PERSISTANT

How do we hear God's voice in the battle cries?

Sometimes it's hard to know what God is calling us to do, especially when we may be fighting against our own fleshly desires to do what we want. We get caught up in life. We can be so bogged down by other emotions that it's hard for us to sift through them to feel the emotions God is wanting us to feel.

"Call to me and I will answer you, and will tell you great and hidden things that you have not known."
Jeremiah 33:3

We must cry out to God during our battles. He will answer us, but we must acknowledge Him above all else. By acknowledging Him, we are letting Him know we are inviting Him into our battles. God can speak through chaos, stillness, defeat, and anger.

God's voice will not remain silent.

Stay persistent in seeking out the voice of the Lord.

Day 5

GOOD FOR THE SOUL

Our love needs to be shown abundantly. When we love others, there should be no boundaries. Our love should be genuine and nonjudgmental. Love should be forgiving and hopeful.

And it is my prayer that your love may abound more and more, with knowledge and all discernment, so that you may approve what is excellent, and so it be pure and blameless for the day of Christ.
Philippians 1:9-10

As we grow toward God, we learn more about what God's love looks like. We learn more about who He is and what He has done. In return, we learn how to love others more like He does. God shows us an abundance of love and grace. He shows us what love is.

When we love like God, we can give others a piece of what God has given us.

Love doesn't always come easy. Sometimes it seems like you must force it. It's hard to love through hurt because betrayal is something that lingers inside of us. It can become deadly to our souls.

We must learn to love, though, just as we learn to forgive. As we become closer to God, we become closer to knowing how to love as He loves us.

Love is just as good for your soul as it is for the one to whom you are showing it.

Day 6

GOD'S APPOINTED TIME

Have you ever felt like God was laying something on your heart? When I started feeling God laying things on my heart, I always wanted to make sure I completely understood; that they weren't selfish desires, but desires from Him. I mean yes, we all have dreams and aspirations, but we should want to be aligned with God's will and not our own. In order for us to do that, it takes time - God's appointed time. It takes prayer and dedication to the vision. It takes discernment.

And the Lord answered me: "Write the vision; make it plain on tablets, so he may run who reads it. For still the vision awaits its appointed time; it hastens to the end – it will not lie. If it seems slow, wait for it; it surely will come; it will not delay." Habakkuk 2:2-3

Write down the things God lays on your heart. In this scripture Habakkuk was told to write clearly and in faith, for what he would write would be used for others in God's appointed time.

Write the things on your heart clearly for you to see. Pray and seek truth over them. Ask God to give you discernment and to align your vision with His will for your life. Continue to be obedient in seeking out what He lays on your heart and patient in waiting for His timing.

If it seems slow, remember God's will does not delay. There is always our time or God's appointed time.

Journal

Day 7

Take time to meditate on God's word. What's on your heart this week?

_____

_____

_____

_____

_____

_____

_____

_____

_____

_____

_____

_____

_____

_____

_____

_____

_____

_____

_____

Week Nineteen

Day 1

HE CALLS US BY NAME

"Fear not, for I have redeemed you; I have called you by name, you are mine." Isaiah 43:1

Imagine yourself in homeroom class for the first time of the school year. The teacher is going through the attendance roll call and she/he calls out each student, name by name. She gets to your name and says, "Insert your name here," and you raise your hand and say present.

Did you know God does the exact same thing with us in many instances in our life? He calls our names out the day He forms us. He calls our names out the day we accept Him. He calls our names out when He specifically appoints us to a greater calling, and He calls our names out the day we meet Him again.

He has called us each individually by name, and He will give us all the choice of raising our hand and saying, "Present." He does this in every situation in our life.

Are we raising our hands high in the presence of the Lord knowing we have already been redeemed?

He has called you out by name, and you are His.

Raise your hands high today in knowing that He is also yours!

Day 2

PERSPECTIVE SHIFT

Sometimes we don't need to ask God for change. We don't need to ask Him to fix our brokenness. We don't need to ask Him to change the situation we are in. Sometimes we just need a perspective shift, to ask God to change our view of what is happening.

I have found that, at times, when I'm trying to fix things, God is saying that it's already been fixed.

What if through our perspective shifts God is trying to teach us something?

> *And may you have the power to understand, as all God's people should, how wide, how long, how high, and how deep his love is.*
> *Ephesians 3:18 (NLT)*

What if you have the wrong point of view in your situation? What if God is just trying to shift your way of thinking? What if He is trying to show you just how much He loves you? Your eyes could just be set on the wrong thing.

Our perspective shift could be just the peace we need to feel God's love the way we were meant to. We may need to realize that God is working through our situation for our good.

Maybe we just need to change our perspective to receive the gift God has for us.

Day 3

WILL OF GOD

Rejection is not an easy word to process when you are on the receiving side of it. Sometime in your life you will feel the sting of rejection. It could be as early as childhood. Rejection can come in many forms: emotional, social, and physical.

In Mark 6 Jesus was teaching in the synagogue with His disciples, and those who heard Him started to question Him, took offense at what He was saying, and rejected who He was. When they did this, He knew it didn't lessen who He was and what He was sent to do.

And he marveled because of their unbelief. And he went about among the villages teaching. Mark 6:6

Rejection is something that can break you down. It's something you can begin to accept. Rejection is not of God and does not come from Him. Think about how many times we still reject the will of God in our lives by living them as we please instead of the way He has called us to.

Whether you have felt rejection before or currently do, I am here to tell you that what others may throw at you as offense is not what God has claimed over you in defense. Rejection can only cause as big of a sting as you allow it. You were made already accepted in the eyes of your Savior. Remember, though, if the worldly rejection hurts us, think about when we refuse heavenly direction from God. Don't reject the will of God in your life.

Day 4

SHAME IS A CHAIN

"Fear not; you will no longer live in shame. Don't be afraid; there is no more disgrace in you. You will no longer remember the shame of your youth and the sorrows of widowhood." Isaiah 54:4 (NLT)

God tells us that He can take away our sorrows and shame. When we repent and lay our sins and shame at the feet of Jesus, we are not to be worried anymore. Our God can renew us and strengthen us when we feel like giving up. He washes away our sins. He makes us whole again within Him. He is our healer and our redeemer.

When we sin, God doesn't want it to burden us. He wants it to teach us, to help us grow, and to make us want to do better so that we may continue our walk with Him. He wants us to learn from our sins and then give them to Him.

No sin was meant to weigh us down. We are not supposed to live in the shame of things we have done wrong. We are to change our ways and remember that God cleanses us. Jesus washed us as white as snow.

Shame is a chain. Allow that chain to be broken by knowing God's promises.

Prayer: Lord we pray that You first forgive us from the sins we have made and might make today. We ask in Your name that You help us to grow through our mistakes and that You surround us with Your mercy.

We praise You now for we know that without You we would be nothing. Because we have a relationship with

You, we are already bound in the love of Your grace and mercy. Thank You, Lord, for giving us second chances, and thank You for taking away our shame. We love You today and every day. Amen

Day 5

HE HAS NO FAVORITES

I'm sure you have a favorite color or maybe even a favorite song. We all get asked those questions at some point. It's an easy conversation starter, especially when you are younger and trying to get to know someone.

In Acts 10 Peter is sent into a trance-like state as he is waiting on food to be prepared. Peter then begins to have a vision.

And there a voice came to him: "Rise, Peter; kill and eat." But Peter said, "By no means, Lord; for I have never eaten anything that is common or unclean." And the voice came to him again a second time, "What God has made clean, do not call common." This happened three times and the thing was taken up at once to heaven.
Acts 10:13-16

"What God has made clean do not call common," or as our generation would say, "Basic." Anyone who has the Lord inside of them and fears Him will be used for His glory here on earth. God calls all of us as believers clean, new, and necessary to deliver His good news. No matter what you've done or haven't done.

So Peter opened his mouth and said: "Truly I understand that God shows no partiality, but in every nation anyone who fears him and does what is right is acceptable to him."
Acts 10:34-35

There is no favoritism shown with God! We are all equal no matter our calling, no matter our background, and no matter our race. God sees us all as His children. If we are

walking in the righteousness of the Lord, we are seen as every other believer. God doesn't choose a favorite; we were all made equal. Division in favoritism comes from the enemy. God doesn't divide; He conquers and pieces together. You and me, He loves us the same!

Day 6

STOP COMPRESSING, LEARN TO EMBRACE

Too often, we numb things, so we don't have to deal with the pain. Instead of dealing with things as they happen, we push them far down inside, compressing them.

Okay guys, I'm getting older. One time in the shower, I actually noticed some varicose veins on the back of my leg. I immediately screamed to my husband, and when he came in (probably thinking I had broken a bone), I looked at him and said, "What is this mess?" As he always does, he more than likely said, "You're so crazy," and walked out. Actually, he immediately ordered me some compression socks, which in return, did not make me feel any more youthful. I was desperate so I'm actually glad he decided to help a girl out.

I ended up wearing those compression socks only twice because they were just so tight that I began thinking I was losing oxygen to my brain.

I could either compress the fact that, yes, I'm getting older, or I could begin to embrace it.

We could also compress the fact that we were really hurt as a child or that we were in a bad relationship. We could compress the fact that we made some extremely bad choices or that we have failed at quite a few things in life. We could compress so much that we really begin to compress ourselves.

*"Whoever wants to embrace life and see the day fill up with good,
Here's what you do: say nothing evil or hurtful; snub evil and cultivate
good; run after peace for all you're worth."*
1 Peter 3:10-11 (MSG)

If we want to embrace life, we have to quit compressing it. We need to snub all the bad stuff and cultivate good things instead. We need to run after the peace intended for our lives and know we are worth it!

Do you know you are worth it? Because you are!

Journal

Day 7

Take time to meditate on God's word. What's on your heart this week?

_____

_____

_____

_____

_____

_____

_____

_____

_____

_____

_____

_____

_____

_____

_____

_____

_____

_____

_____

_____

Week Twenty

Day 1

WORKING FOR MY CREATOR

We all have a job, whether it's working an 8-5 or it's taking care of our kids/home. Some of us even pull double duty at times and do both. In the grand scheme, we are all working for the same things - pleasing and serving God.

So, my dear brothers and sisters, be strong and immovable. Always work enthusiastically for the Lord, for you know that nothing you do for the Lord is ever useless.
1 Corinthians 15:58 (NLT)

I once heard someone teach on this very thing, and when times get tough at my job, I try to remind myself of it.

You are not working for man; you are working for God. In all that you do and all that you say, you should be pleasing Him and not others.

We can apply this even when doing our house duties as well. The next time we get frustrated with doing a lot around the house, we can remind ourselves that we aren't doing these things just for our families. We do them to be pleasing to God. God sees our sacrifices, dedication, and hard work in all we do. Remember, He is our ultimate reward.

When we are pleasing the Lord in our actions and thoughts, we are subsequently pleasing to everyone else around us. God wants us to be laborers for Him. We were put here to be His hands and feet in all that we do.

Remember today and every day that God sees and knows

our hearts. When we are willing to be used in the smallest of things, He can then be more willing to use us elsewhere.

Be strong and dedicated to your faith and know that when you are working for the Lord it is never useless!

Day 2

HANDLE WITH CARE

It's hard when life hits you with unexpected things that are difficult to understand. It's hard to control our emotions and our thoughts from running wild.

Trust in the Lord with all your heart, and lean not on your own understanding. In all your ways acknowledge him, and he will make straight your paths. Proverbs 3:5-6

God didn't send His son to die to save us for us not to trust His process. God is the beginning and the end. His love is bigger than any situation that may arise in our lives.

When we face life-altering situations, God is there. He is waiting for us to turn to Him, allowing Him to witness inside our souls. We cannot handle things without God.

God wants us to hit our knees in prayer and sing him praises. He wants us to trust Him. Everything is not meant for us to understand. Our difficult circumstances weren't meant for us to try and handle or face alone. The Bible says "acknowledge" God through those times and know He is there, and He will direct your paths.

Emotions are okay. Feeling sad, triumphant, and hurt is part of being human. It's okay to be sad about your situation, but don't dwell in the sadness. Know that you are a child of the One True King. Find God's embrace today in your hurt. Allow Him to take your feelings and fill your heart with love.

Day 3

FRUIT OF THE SPIRIT

We would love for everything to be perfect in our lives, for nothing to go wrong and no bad things to come our way. However, if we stayed on a mountaintop forever without purpose, we would become stagnant and leave unfulfilled what God wanted to do in us.

As I was writing, I thought that there must be something in the valley that you don't see on the mountaintop.

Then I found this quote, "Mountaintops are for views and inspiration, but fruit is grown in the valleys." - Billy Graham

It's not that God can't be seen on the mountaintop, but without the valleys our view of Him would be off.

As much as we don't want bad things to happen to our families and pray for them to go away when they do, we can find joy in knowing that they can bring an abundance of fruit.

Fruit is what's needed for us to remain humble when we are on the mountaintop. Fruit is substantial for our growth.

But the fruit of the Spirit is love, joy, peace, patience, kindness, faithfulness, gentleness, self-control; against such things there is no law.
Galatians 5:22-23

In the valleys, we must exhibit the fruit of the Spirit so that on the mountaintops we can rejoice in the One who brought us through the valley. God is our guide in our lows

and our highs. If we aren't being led by Him, then the mountaintops won't even seem like mountaintops. Instead, we will hit a plateau even on the mountain.

Each valley comes with great fruit to be used on the mountain.

Day 4

BURN YOUR LIGHT BRIGHT

The light shines in the darkness, and the darkness has not overcome it.
John 1:5

When we have God's light illuminating our paths, no darkness can overcome it.

Your word is a lamp to my feet and the light to my path.
Psalm 119:105

Since His word is a lamp for our feet and a light unto our paths, when we have Him within our hearts, we will always overcome the things that are set before us. When our path is lit by the word of the Lord, the hardships and distractions may come, but they won't be able to put out what is burning bright for Jesus Christ.

Make sure you are allowing your light to shine as brightly as possible. Fuel your lamp with praise, with reading your Bible, and through prayer. Keep your light shining bright for all to see.

He is the lamp that lights our way in this dark world. God is our direction and our purpose. Be a light unto this world and allow Jesus to light your path for others to see. When your light is shining, you have no idea whose path you may come across, and they too may be led to the light of salvation through Jesus, our Savior.

Light up the world with your love for Jesus Christ today and always!

Day 5

WHAT SEEDS ARE
YOU WATERING?

When God's word comes down, it does not come down empty. God sends messages to us all the time. He sends deliverance to our situations and to our minds. Our surroundings can be reflections of that joy.

If then you have been raised with Christ, seek the things that are above, where Christ is, seated at the right hand of God. Set your minds on things that are above, not on things that are on earth.
Colossians 3:1-2

When we seek the Lord, that is where growth begins. We must be fully aware of what the devil is capable and keep our minds and thoughts on what God is sending us. We must change our ways by changing our thoughts.

We need to make sure we are always watering the right seed and feeding the right things. God has invited us to come and think as He does. We need to seek Him first above all else. Go to Him before anyone else. Ask Him to change your way of thinking so that it's set only on Him.

We don't want to grow any thoughts that He didn't send.

Day 6

EXTEND AN INVITE

How many times do we invite Jesus into where we are? Do you invite Him to come into your place of work before you go in? What about inviting Him into your home before you get there, or even if you are just walking into a restaurant to eat and saying, "Jesus, I'm inviting You to go with me, to eat with me, to protect me, and to keep me safe."

I don't think it's really a habit for us to invite Jesus to go with us. We just assume that He is already there, but I think that Jesus wants to feel welcome just like anybody else.

Because he has inclined his ear to me, therefore I will call on Him as long as I live. Psalm 116:2

Satan is real, but (there always is a but) God has much more power - much more power and way more authority. You see, Satan is weak and can only claim what you give him when he comes to attack. God is strong, and even without us giving Him things, He still will claim victory over them.

We forget when times begin to become a struggle, or even when things seem to be going well, that we must always claim the blood of Jesus. Sometimes it's just as important to shout the Lord's name over and over as it is to pray in His name.

JESUS, JESUS, JESUS!

It's not just "call on Him," it needs to also be "call to Him." Call Him into your situation. Invite Him to come everywhere you go. Make Him feel just as welcome every

day as you do when you try to pray things away. Jesus, you are always invited here!

Journal

Day 7

Take time to meditate on God's word. What's on your heart this week?

_____

_____

_____

_____

_____

_____

_____

_____

_____

_____

_____

_____

_____

_____

_____

_____

_____

_____

_____

_____

Week Twenty-One

Day 1

YOU WERE CREATED FOR

A lot of us are continually seeking our purpose/calling in life. I think when we realize for whom we were created, it becomes a game changer.

For in him all things were created: things in heaven and on earth, visible and invisible, whether thrones or powers or rulers or authorities; all things have been created through him and for him.
Colossians 1:16 (NIV)

Do you realize the significance of remembering for whom you were created? For a long time, I can say I didn't. You see, if we remember that we were created for God, we wouldn't seek only the things that make us happy. We would have a heart for pleasing God. A heart that was continually seeking and going after the One we were created for, knowing that in Him is the only place we will find what we were created to do.

Figuring out and always remembering that we were created for God gives us the purpose for which we all go searching. If you were created for God, then no matter where you are right now, you have been put into purpose.

How can God use you right where you are? Wherever you are in life you are able to share the gospel of Christ. God created you for this moment. You have been created in Him, through Him, and for Him. That is your purpose right now and every day. How can you live for Him in your right now?

Day 2

BALANCING YOUR WALK

Battles will come and go. There will be the lies the enemy tells you, and then there will sometimes be the fear of the unknown as you wait.

For I, the Lord your God, hold your right hand; it is I who say to you,
"Fear not, I am the one who helps you."
Isaiah 41:13

Some days will be better than others, and some days the enemy will get a hold of a thought or feeling and just won't let go. Sometimes the enemy's tricks, hacks, and schemes that we fight last just too long. We seek out what's hurting us more than we should. Some of the pressures just come from ourselves. The enemy could be there to push the thought of them more, but our human agenda can sometimes just be downright unbalanced.

You shall seek those who contend with you, but you shall not find
them; those who war against you shall be as nothing at all.
Isaiah 41:12

The Lord holds our hand and goes to battle for us. Life's obstacles may be stumbling blocks for us but not for Him. He will balance your walk and protect your fall.

Don't seek out the lies. Seek the truth in God. The truth in His word. Don't spend time contending with people or things. Those things that bring wrath against you are "nothing at all."

Day 3

WE TOO OVERCAME

How do I overcome what's trying to overcome me?

My thoughts sometimes run rampant, and it becomes plain to see that I start to hunger for Your word to begin to engulf me.

Those tender moments when I set out to bask in the forgiveness You offered though I thought it was my last.

Seconds of fight, struggle to breathe,
the breaths began to become way too deep.

Deeper from within a place hard to explain,
a place where You had showed up to call me out by name.

You said my child I am here for all your fear and doubt,
to take over those hidden feelings you sometimes shout.

There isn't anything that He can't do,
that's when He begins to show us that we were made anew.

Creation with a purpose and a driven plan,
to help push others into His promise land.

We can't give authority to what He hasn't claimed,
for when He overcame the grave,

WE TOO OVERCAME!

We have been given hope through His word even when our

minds may not understand. It's not our job to decipher His greater plans.

We need to remember to keep our faith strong in our Father's hands.

> *Finally, be strong in the Lord and in his mighty power.*
> *Ephesians 6:10 (NIV)*

For what He has set forth for you,
the enemy cannot devour!

(This was a poem I wrote remembering God's faithfulness through all the trials. It's something maybe you can relate to if you have ever been through a hard time or are in one now. God overcame the grave so that we too could overcome.)

Day 4

SECURITY BLANKET

Everyone loves a sense of security. A sense of feeling held, feeling taken care of, being in a safe place, being stable, or feeling free.

With men, a lot of times, it's their job or supplying for their family that is their security. With women, most of the time, it's about safety and stability. Either way, security is a huge part of our everyday life, even with Jesus and our faith.

As women, if we feel insecure or unsafe in our own homes, we get scared. If men, on the other hand, are feeling unstable in their ability to provide, they get scared. It's fear of the unknown.

Our security can't be found in the unknown, though. It's found in the living, eternal God. Our security is found in our salvation and hope through Jesus Christ.

"The eternal God is your dwelling place, and underneath are the everlasting arms. And he thrust out the enemy before you, and said, 'Destroy.'" Deuteronomy 33:27

Our God is our safe place, our stability, and our freedom. He holds us, and He provides. He is our security blanket always. He protects us from the unknown and casts out all the enemy may form.

With whatever you may be going through, find your security under His everlasting arms. We can be secure in Him!

Day 5

BEAUTY IN THE PROCESS

Have you ever stopped to think about all of God's creations, the big ones and the small ones?! How He intricately and delicately made it all? How He knew exactly what He wanted and how He wanted it?

Have you ever thought that that is exactly what He did with us? He knew the world, and He knew that He wanted us in it. He knew that He wanted us here. So, he decided to make us just as we are.

For by him all things were created, in heaven and on earth, visible and invisible, whether thrones or dominions or rulers or authorities - all things were created through him and for him. Colossians 1:16

Maybe we need to stop and appreciate the beauty in it. The beauty in the process. The beauty in us. The beauty in all His creations. There is beauty all around us that stays unrecognized because of our inability to see it due to us keeping our lives too filled with things and not enough God.

Take time today and slow down. Try to see the things you've never seen before. Spend time with God in a quiet place. Compliment someone. Our lives are short. Things change, but God's love remains the same. Don't miss out on the beauty He created in you and the beauty he created in the world.

Slow down and take it all in.

Day 6

BUILDING YOU

Too often we forget God's power. We forget just how mighty He is.

Let's set the scenario. There were two men traveling down the road to Emmaus after the Crucifixion and Resurrection of Christ.

That very day two of them were going to a village named Emmaus, about seven miles from Jerusalem, and they were talking with each other about all these things that had happened. While they were talking and discussing together, Jesus himself drew near and went with them. But their eyes were kept from recognizing him. And he said to them, "What is the conversation you are holding with each other as you walk?" And they stood still looking sad.
Luke 24:13-17

How many times in our own life are our eyes blind to recognizing God in our situations? Sometimes when He speaks to us or shows us what we need, we still look sad in our circumstance because it may not be what we want. We are slow in accepting where God has put us or the positions we are in because we may not feel comfortable or willing to be there. Too many times, we are blind to seeing God in our places right now. We are too busy looking for the places we want to be. The right now is the blessing you don't want to be too blind to see God in. God is your blessing in disguise right where you are.

Don't miss what God has for you in the right now by being worried about the past or what you thought was supposed

to happen. The buildup is the plan to build you closer to Him. Closer to His kingdom.

Was it not necessary that the Christ should suffer these things and enter into his glory? Luke 24:26

Is it not necessary for us to do the same? Sometimes His glory may be in the suffering. Have you ever thought that amidst the pain He's preparing us to accept the blessing the way we were meant to? Without the process there would be no celebration.

Journal

Day 7

Take time to meditate on God's word. What's on your heart this week?

_____

_____

_____

_____

_____

_____

_____

_____

_____

_____

_____

_____

_____

_____

_____

_____

_____

_____

Week Twenty-Two

Day 1

WE ALL HAVE CHOICES

Each day we make new choices. Do you think you always pick God first? Every day we should allow our choices to be guided by God. When we commit to having a relationship with God, we are allowing ourselves to be faithful in what we know is true. When we seek God's kingdom first, all our needs will be supplied to us. This is what the Bible says:

"But seek first the kingdom of God and his righteousness, and all these things will be added to you." Matthew 6:33

When we rise each morning, we have a choice to speak to God. Throughout our day, we have a choice to rely on God. At night, we make a choice to pray to God. We are full of choices to live for Him and put Him first or to live for ourselves. Who are you living for?

We have the audacity to call people selfish and self-centered, but then when we look in the mirror, have we truly faced who we are? We have no right to claim these things over someone if we aren't even willing to claim them over ourselves. Can you imagine if God thought those things about us every time, we chose the phone over our Bibles, sleeping in over church, or TV over prayer? I'm guilty....

Thank goodness our God doesn't judge us the way we see fit to judge others at times. I am thankful He allows us more time to put Him first and lots of tries to figure it out.

Day 2

MARVEL IN HIS GOODNESS TODAY

But Peter rose and ran to the tomb; stooping and looking in, he saw the linen cloths by themselves; and he went home marveling at what had happened. Luke 24:12

Has God ever done something for you that made you marvel at what had happened? In this verse, Jesus had risen from the tomb just as God had promised would happen.

I can remember a time when I would marvel at the fact that I owned my own home. I would pull out of the driveway and look back at it and just thank God for how he had moved in my life. It was simply all because of how he loved me and promised that he'd take care of me. It was such a blessing. He always promises to take care of his children.

I just love this verse and how it says Peter marveled over what had happened. Peter knew what he was capable of. We do too. We serve a God with endless possibilities and a God who loves us more than we can comprehend!

Today, take some time and just marvel at the ways God has worked in your life, the small and big ways he's moved mountains and made things a possibility for you. He has walked with you, cared for you, and fulfilled promises that otherwise couldn't be filled.

Thank Him for being your Father and have a grateful heart today.

Day 3

FINDING PEACE

"You keep him in perfect peace whose mind is stayed on you, because he trusts in you." Isaiah 26:3

Finding peace within you is something you can't do by yourself. Peace comes from a relationship with God. Peace lies within your heart and comes from a depth of understanding and trust. When we allow God to take over our lives in the way we live and how we choose to handle things, we have peace. We must gain a peaceful heart through knowing Jesus Christ.

God can take over our lives and grant us a heart full of peace when we listen and obey his commands. Peace is handing yourself over and allowing God to do the rest. Peace is the ultimate trust, not in you, but in your creator.

Peace means freedom from disturbance; quiet and tranquility.

Maybe to have the peace your heart needs, you need to get quiet. Getting quiet with God allows you to breathe. It allows rest, and it allows peace.

God wants us to have a peaceful heart. One that is strong within Him. Even in a world full of distractions, we remain calm because He remains our center. Sometimes getting still is getting to know the peace you need.

Day 4

BASKET FOR CHRIST

Ever heard of the saying, "Don't put all your eggs in one basket?" I started thinking yesterday about this saying, and I think it couldn't be further from the truth. The meaning of the saying is to not concentrate all your prospects and resources in one place or thing. Honestly though, as a believer, I want all my eggs to be in one basket, and that's the basket of Christ. If all my eggs are in His basket, I live with a basket of truth and fullness.

We get so caught up trying to sift through what eggs we have and where to place them. Time, money, and people could be a few. How do we keep up with everything and manage it? What we don't realize is that when life becomes overwhelming, the wrong basket is probably getting full, and we are losing sight of the basket we are meant to keep overflowing. The truth is when our eggs are in God's basket, His hand is always on them.

Instead of "don't put all your eggs in one basket," I think we need to make sure our eggs are in the right basket. When our eggs are placed in the right basket, the basket of Christ, we will have what we need and the desires of our hearts.

What basket are you placing your eggs in? God's basket offers hope, deliverance, forgiveness, mercy, grace, peace, happiness, and love.

To you, O Lord, I lift up my soul. O my God, in you I trust; let me not be put to shame; let not my enemies exult over me. Psalm 25:1-2

Day 5

GIVE IT ALL AWAY

We search and search for answers when we want to know the truth about something or someone. We may ask God for direction or for Him to reveal something to us. Searching for something ourselves can become tiring and start to wear our minds and bodies out. It becomes draining. It's much like a race to a finish line of truth, but we have no clue where that finish line even is.

Instead of searching for answers or wondering what to do, we need to give it all to God. Seeking the truth in Him is what sets us free from being captive in our own thoughts.

The truth is in his word. The answers come from giving things up to dig deeper into Him. Sometimes, just sometimes, all it takes is allowing ourselves to stop searching for what may not be obtainable, and instead search for God in the right now. He will reveal what needs to be seen because He is the TRUTH and the LIGHT.

Seek the Lord and his strength; seek his presence continually!
1 Chronicles 16:11

Day 6

HEALING NEEDS TO TAKE PLACE

When Jesus saw him lying there and knew that he had already been there a long time, he said to him, "Do you want to be healed?" The sick man answered him, "Sir, I have no one to put me into the pool when the water is stirred up, and while I am going another steps down before me." Jesus said to him, "Get up, take up your bed, and walk." And at once the man was healed, and he took up his bed and walked.
John 5:6-9

What excuses are you making to not follow God and do what He is laying on your heart? There is healing that needs to take place within you and for your life.

Don't let the healing slip by because you're afraid to take the step!

Sometimes it's in our obedient seasons that God is working on our healing.

You need to start believing in what He can do and stop having the mentality that you can't. You may be fighting the same thing for years. This man fought his sickness for 38 years. You may be wondering where your healing is.

Don't look for it in your excuses, it will never be found.

Take shelter under the One who can make you walk again. God has claimed the victory over your healing. Just as Jesus said to this man, we must GET UP. He wants us to claim power over our healing and walk!

Journal

Day 7

Take time to meditate on God's word. What's on your heart this week?

_____

_____

_____

_____

_____

_____

_____

_____

_____

_____

_____

_____

_____

_____

_____

_____

_____

_____

Week Twenty-Three

Day 1

BE OPENED

What does it mean to need God? It could look a little different for each of us in whatever we may be going through. I thought to myself one night, "I want to need Him, whatever needing Him may look like."

Two stories I read in Mark 7 were about Jesus healing a woman's daughter by casting out a demon and healing a deaf man that also had a speech impediment (Mark 7:24-37). When healing the deaf man Jesus said some words that really stuck with me.

And looking up to heaven, he sighed and said to him, "Ephphatha," that is, "Be opened." And his ears were opened, his tongue was released, and he spoke plainly. Mark 7:34-35

Be opened; "Ephphatha." He said these words to this man in healing. When we need God to move, don't we also need to be Ephphatha? We need to "be opened" to what needing him looks like. The need for Jesus came in what they wanted Jesus to take away. The woman and the man both needed healing in different areas of their life, but because they needed that healing they had "the need" for Jesus. Without the healing we may not see the need as clearly.

So, I say to myself that I want to need Him whatever needing Him may look like. It could be that in the healing we see just how much we need Him. Ephphatha; "Be opened." Let's be opened to what He is doing, knowing that in the healing may be right where we find and get to know Him the most!

Day 2

OUT OF YOUR HANDS

Have you ever read something, and it stepped all over your toes?

Do you trust God when His answer is, "Wait"?

Prayers often don't get answered immediately, and oftentimes God must work through a situation for the purpose to be revealed on the other side of it. Are we going to trust God through it, or are we going to fall when the going gets tough?

We can be quick to fall when things seem out of our hands. We want to try to pick up the pieces and get them back into our control, back into our grasp. It's difficult to realize that we really have no control in the first place.

When we realize that the things, we assume we have control over are better off out of our hands and in the hands of God, our burdens start to be lifted.

Those who know your name trust in you, for you, Lord, have never forsaken those who seek you. Psalm 9:10 (NIV)

God has a far better purpose and plan for your life than anything you could come up with.

Day 3

RIGHT IN FRONT OF YOU

"Look among the nations, and see; wonder and be astounded. For I am doing a work in your days that you would not believe if told."
Habakkuk 1:5

Isn't it so good to know that if we look around, we may not be able to see it, but God is doing such a work inside us and around us that we wouldn't even believe it if He told us? I love the first words in this scripture, "Look, among."

So many times, I ride along the same roads and all of a sudden notice something I've never seen before because I have never actually looked. What if we just took the time to look deeper into our own lives and look deeper into others? What if we looked for the things God is trying to show us and tried to see them the way He has intended?

Look today. Open your eyes and try to see what God has planted right in front of you.

Day 4

TELL HIM SOMETHING

I was once reminded by a sweet little seven-year-old that sometimes we just need to tell God something.

How many times do we get stuck in funks or in moods where we feel far from Him, but He is always tailing us and wondering if we will just tell Him something? He is our Father, but He is also our friend.

Thus the Lord used to speak to Moses face to face, as a man speaks to his friend. Exodus 33:11

The Lord is near us always. We probably feel we hear from Him more when we are brokenhearted, but He is near us always. He is willing and ready for us to tell Him something. He is waiting for us to pour out our hearts to Him and speak to Him. It doesn't have to just be in prayer. Talk to Him like you do a friend. He is always waiting to hear from you.

Tell Him something today.

Day 5

SERVANT OF THE LORD

"For nothing will be impossible with God." And Mary said, "Behold,
I am the servant of the Lord; let it be to me according to your word."
And the angel departed from her.
Luke 1:37-38

This is when Mary is told by an angel that she will birth the Messiah, and that Elizabeth, who has not been able to conceive, will also bear a child.

Today, we can easily get caught up in doubt, worry, or even just the need for more. We serve such a supernatural God with the ability to provide all things. I love how in this verse Mary accepts what God is giving her. It made me think that I want to be more like Mary. She was bold. She was brave. She said, "Behold, I am the servant of the Lord; let it be to me according to your word." Are we not all servants of the Lord here to live out what He has called of us? I want to be more accepting of whatever that may be. Nothing is impossible with God. He sees the need for you just as He saw the need to send his Son into the world years ago. He was a faithful, giving, ever-so-present God then and He is ever-so-present now. If He saw the need then, He sees your needs now.

Do you accept that you are a servant of the Lord and that He has chosen you according to his word? He has chosen you to be loved and to be cherished. To be free from need.

Nothing is impossible with God!

Day 6

WHAT CAN YOU GIVE?

We have the luxury of so much, and as the years go on, that luxury will grow to be more. We can get caught up in living for the riches of the world or living in the riches of the Savior. It reminds me of the story of the rich man and Lazarus in Luke.

"There was a rich man who was clothed in purple and fine linen and who feasted sumptuously every day. And at his gate was laid a poor man named Lazarus, covered with sores, who desired to be fed with what fell from the rich man's table. Moreover, even the dogs came and licked his sores. The poor man died and was carried by the angels to Abraham's side. The rich man also died and was buried, and in Hades, being in torment, he lifted up his eyes and saw Abraham far off and Lazarus at this side. And he called out, 'Father Abraham, have mercy on me, and send Lazarus to dip the end of his finger in the water and cool my tongue, for I am in anguish in this flame. But Abraham said, 'Child, remember that you in your lifetime received your good things, and Lazarus in like manner bad things; but now he is comforted here, and you are in anguish." Luke 16:19-25

Lazarus desired to be fed from the luxury of the rich man's table, but he wouldn't feed him even though he was there every day. The rich man was living in the luxury of what he had and not in what he could give. His heart was closed from seeing the true luxury that's in our Savior. You can have everything, but it still will not satisfy your hearts desires the way that God will. The way that living a life with a heart full of God will. The way doing things that aren't seen will. We can find our greater value or placement here on earth or in the riches of heaven. The real luxury lies in what's in the center of your heart.

Journal

Day 7

Take time to meditate on God's word. What's on your heart this week?

_____

_____

_____

_____

_____

_____

_____

_____

_____

_____

_____

_____

_____

_____

_____

_____

_____

Week Twenty-Four

Day 1

TRY AGAIN

Too many times in our life, we allow failure to dictate our faith. Failure doesn't mean we should quit. Failing or making mistakes doesn't mean we should stop. The word "failure" means the lack of success. To lack something means to not to have enough of something. Maybe failure makes it seem like you are lacking God, but God is the success of failure. True failure is only when you don't get back up and try again. There are many people in the Bible that felt like they had failed. The first that comes to my mind is Peter. He fished and fished and came back with nothing, but at the first sight of lacking, he didn't quit. Jesus ended up blessing him with many fish.

I can do all things through him who strengthens me.
Philippians 4:13

I can do nothing on my own.
John 5:30

With God we lack nothing. We are going to fall, and we are going to feel as if it's too hard to get back up. However, the first thought in the fall should be, "I am not lacking. I have God." You can't allow the fall to keep you down. Put your eyes on God, and remember He is success. God sees your heart and the desires of it.

Day 2

COME IN HUMILITY

It's not about how much we do for the Lord, it's the way we do it that matters. God doesn't see the amount, He sees the humility. One person could just pray every so often, and another serve in a multitude of ways but boast in them. God isn't about what you do, He just wants you to do it in humility.

This is the parable of the Pharisee and the Tax Collector:

"Two men went up to the temple to pray, one a Pharisee and the other a tax collector. The Pharisee stood by himself and prayed: 'God, I thank you that I am not like other people—robbers, evildoers, adulterers—or even like this tax collector. I fast twice a week and give a tenth of all I get.' "But the tax collector stood at a distance. He would not even look up to heaven, but beat his breast and said, 'God, have mercy on me, a sinner.' "I tell you that this man, rather than the other, went home justified before God. For all those who exalt themselves will be humbled, and those who humble themselves will be exalted."
Luke 18:10-14

We are all sinners. It doesn't matter the sin. God looks at our hearts and the manner in which we come to Him. Is it in a boastful manner, or are we coming with humility? Accepting of what we know, we are but asking for Him to be merciful on us. Even the "other men, extortioners, unjust, adulterers, and the tax collector" can be forgiven and be new creations in God. Those titles are just titles and not the name He will write down in His book. Do all that you do in humility, whatever it may be, seeking God first over all else.

Day 3

CHILDLIKE FAITH

*"Truly I say to you, whoever does not receive the kingdom of God like
a child shall not enter it."*
Luke 18:17

We've heard the saying, "Having a childlike faith." This is a
faith where you are not prideful but mindful. A faith where
you are teachable, willing to learn, and not set in your ways.
A childlike faith is being in the background of your Father
and allowing Him to work. To me, receiving the kingdom
of God like a child means to know where you stand with
God. Lowering yourself to know that He is the authority
and ruler over you and your life. Having the wisdom to try
and live in humility, and to know that you can't do life
without Him.

Children are constantly learning from their parents. They
are constantly taking things in and building themselves from
it. When you are a child, you trust and believe that the
person who is there is going to take care of you. Children
just believe without hesitation.

That is how we should receive the kingdom of God; as a
child believing without hesitation that He will take care of
us. He is for us. We are building ourselves with the truth
of His kingdom.

Day 4

SUBMIT TO GOD

Time doesn't stand still, but neither does our God. If you are anything like me, I look at my children all the time and wonder where the time has gone. If you don't have children, I am sure you reminisce about a time in your life and think about how fast time has gone by. We all get to an age when we start wondering how time goes by so fast.

Time surely doesn't stand still, but thankfully neither does our God. If only we could truly have five more minutes. Five more minutes when we are running late in the morning. Five more minutes to sleep in. Five more minutes with loved ones or five more minutes to just get life right at times.

What if I told you that you have those five more minutes right now to change something? You have five minutes right now to put your faith over the matter of your mind. Allow what God has claimed over your day to overpower anything that may not be sent from Him. Are you running late? It's okay. Are you angry about something from yesterday? Drop it. You have those five minutes right now to change your course of action for the day, from your thoughts to your actions. You can change what happens going forward, whether you move forward in fear or in faith.

In all your ways submit to him, and he will make your paths straight.
Proverbs 3:6 (NIV)

Adding Jesus and submitting to Him are totally different. We can just add Him to our day, or we can submit to His

will for our day and know that no matter what has happened or is going to happen, His will is perfect and complete over our lives. We accept it and allow Him to move. Time may not stand still, but our God doesn't either. Whatever He has for you is far greater than you can imagine. Just submit your life to Him.

Day 5

YOU HAVE A STORY

I found that there are around 255 stories in the Bible. This is just an estimate, but it gives us an idea of how many people's stories we have that show us who God is and what He did through His Son, our Savior, Jesus Christ.

Did you realize that you have a story, too? A story of God's redeeming love; a story of God's deliverance in your own life. Have you ever thought about your story?

Honestly, I used to be so upset about mine. I used to ask God why He chose me for my story. Why I was the one that had to go through some of the things I did as a child. Why I couldn't have had a more peaceful story. Until one day, I finally realized my story was so much more than just things I had to go through. My story was purposeful and full of God's grace and mercy.

We must own our stories. Our stories are glimpses for others to see how truly good our God is. Our stories can be hope, strength, and even the encouragement someone needs to push through theirs. Our stories are what God has given us, and that's the promise for eternal life through His Son, Jesus.

Own your story.

And this is the testimony, that God gave us eternal life, and this life is in his Son. 1 John 5:11

Day 6

WHAT ARE WE GIVING TO GOD?

And Gad came that day to David and said to him, "Go up, raise an altar to the Lord on the threshing floor of Araunah the Jebusite." So David went up at Gad's word, as the Lord commanded. And when Araunah looked down, he saw the king and his servants coming on toward him. And Araunah went out and paid homage to the king with his face to the ground. And Araunah said, "Why has my lord the king come to his servant?" David said, "To buy the threshing floor from you, in order to build an altar to the Lord, that the plague may be averted from the people." Then Araunah said to David, "Let my lord the king take and offer up what seems good to him. Here are the oxen for the burnt offering and the threshing sledges and the yokes of the oxen for the wood. All this, O king, Araunah gives to the king." And Araunah said to the king, "May the Lord your God accept you." But the king said to Araunah, "No, but I will buy it from you for a price. I will not offer burnt offerings to the Lord my God that cost me nothing." So David bought the threshing floor and the oxen for fifty shekels of silver. And David built there an altar to the Lord and offered burnt offerings and peace offerings. So the Lord responded to the plea for the land, and the plague was averted from Israel.
2 Samuel 24:18-25

This scripture is about sacrifice and what sacrifice may cost you. David says he wouldn't take it all for free. He will pay for the offerings for His Lord. He wanted the offerings to cost him something.

A lot of times, we want to offer God the minimum that we can give Him. "Lord, I don't have time to take a few minutes to devote to You, but I'll try and pray before bed." "Lord, I'm busy with my day, but at the first sight of need I will come to You." "Lord, I really want to read my Bible,

but I just don't understand it." "Lord, there just isn't enough time in the day, but when I find the time, I will give You some of it."

Sacrifice for the Lord comes at the cost of something to you.

That's what God sees. "Instead of sleeping ten more minutes, I'll get up and pray." "Instead of taking this twenty to go out to eat, I will put it in the offering plate." "Instead of just not taking time to read the Bible, I can start off with a learning one that breaks it down, so I can understand it better."

We are here to sacrifice for God, and those sacrifices come at a cost. They will take some of our time, money, or energy.

This is Him allowing us to choose to give back to Him.

Journal

Day 7

Take time to meditate on God's word. What's on your heart this week?

_____

_____

_____

_____

_____

_____

_____

_____

_____

_____

_____

_____

_____

_____

_____

_____

_____

_____

_____

_____

_____

_____

Week Twenty-Five

Day 1

IN THE WILDERNESS

Have you ever found yourself in the wilderness, or do you feel like you are there now? I mean wilderness figuratively, but if I were literally lost in the woods, what would I do? I would have to call out to the Lord; I truly couldn't make it on my own. We sometimes get lost in the wilderness in our own body, mind, and spirit. We feel lost in everyday life. Maybe you are going on day to day, but you are just getting by. Every one of us has been through times when we were lost in a place or situation, not knowing which way to go to get out. If you find yourself lost in your own wilderness, call out to God.

God is and will be the only place you can turn to get you where you need to be.

"The voice of one crying in the wilderness: 'Prepare the way of the Lord, make his paths straight. Every valley shall be filled, and every mountain and hill shall be made low, and the crooked shall become straight, and the rough places shall become level ways, and all flesh shall see the salvation of God.'" Luke 3:4-6

Everything can be made right with God. When we "prepare the way of the Lord" in our lives, He can do a work like never before. He can move any mountain and straighten any road. You may be lost in the wilderness now, but you won't stay there with the salvation of God.

Day 2

GOD'S VIEW

They used to have these things on doors called peepholes. From the inside you could see a wide-angle view of what was on the outside. If you looked in from the outside, you couldn't see a thing.

That's a lot like God's view on our own lives. God being on the inside seeing exactly what's happening and the course of action that must take place. He sees a wide-angle view into everything. We are remaining on the other side without a clear sight of what He has planned. If we trust in the One who has the ability to open the door, no plan will go unfulfilled. Everything will come out to be perfect and complete in His hands.

Are you in the process of waiting for God to answer the door? If you trust in Him, at the right time that door will open, and you will then see the masterpiece he has created through that tiny hole on the other side.

But I trust in you, O Lord; I say, "You are my God."
Psalm 31:14

Day 3

BE BOLD

We know the enemy comes to kill, steal, and destroy. He will prowl like a roaring lion looking for what he can devour. He knows your weaknesses. He wants to take your boldness and make you timid and scared of the unknown. He wants you to allow your mind to become weak and replace God's love that He has claimed over you. The enemy makes you feel as if your ability to overcome or resist your temptations or weaknesses are out of your control. He will have you believe that if you have fallen, you've failed; however, failure doesn't come from the fall, it comes from giving up and not trying again.

For the spirit God gave us does not make us timid, but gives us power, love and self-discipline.
2 Timothy 1:7 (NIV)

"For the spirit God gave us...."

He gave us a spirit of boldness, of power, of love and self-control.

God gave us a spirit that doesn't make us timid but allows us to be bold. He made us courageous and confident in Him. He gave us a spirit of power to overcome. He gave us a spirit of love to be filled with His love and to love others. He gave us a spirit to know we are loved and a spirit of self-discipline. Even if our hands may not feel in control, they are controlled by His. He gave these things to us. These feelings, these emotions, these words to claim over ourselves. Are we allowing ourselves to receive that free gift?

Day 4

SHOULDERS BACK

As a little girl I can always remember my grandma saying, "Stand tall, make sure to push your shoulders back, have good posture." At the time, I would l think to myself, "Why does it matter if my shoulders are down or my posture isn't good?" I've come to realize now, though, that my grandma always wanted me to be confident in who I was and where I was going. It wasn't all for the purpose of posture, but because she knew when I allowed myself to not stand tall with my shoulders back, I was also allowing my head to fall. I would begin to focus on the ground more and wasn't looking where I was going.

I say this because God also wants us to be confident in our faith and in our walk. He wants us to be confident in who He is and what He has come to do for us. He wants us to stand tall with our shoulders back, our head looking forward and not down. He wants our eyes to be focused on Him. Different body language could be all we need to walk in God's confidence for ourselves.

Let us then approach God's throne of grace with confidence, so that we may receive mercy and find grace to help us in our time of need.
Hebrews 4:16 (NIV)

Let us approach God with confidence today. We can be confident in Him knowing who He is and all that He has already done.

Day 5

TAKE A ROLL CALL

Remember roll call in school? If you were there, you'd raise your hand and say, "Present," and if you weren't, they would mark you absent because there wouldn't be an answer from anyone. Every time you do a roll call with God asking Him if He is here, there will never be a time that He will not say, "Present!" Our God is always available. He always shows up, and as cliché as it may sound, He is always right on time.

God is our refuge and strength, a very present help in trouble. Therefore we will not fear though the earth gives way, though the mountains be moved into the heart of the sea. Psalm 46:1-2

Whenever you are facing fear of an outcome, fear of the future, or fear of a situation or a decision, God is present. What's around you may seem absent, but what's in front of you is ever-so-present. When it may seem that the earth is giving way, or you feel all alone, take a roll call. Others may not be there, but the One that matters will always be. God loves when we call out His name. That means we are humbling ourselves before Him knowing that we can't do it alone.

Next time you are fearful of the future, take a roll call.

Day 6

WALK IN THE SPIRIT

As children, we struggle with wanting approval from our parents and friends. As we get older, we start to struggle with wanting the same approval from others or even ourselves. Authenticity is what God created for you. He made you perfect in His image.

There is therefore now no condemnation for those who are in Christ Jesus. For the law of the Spirit of life has set you free in Christ Jesus from the law of sin and death. For God has done what the law, weakened by the flesh, could not do. By sending his own Son in the likeness of sinful flesh and for sin, he condemned sin in the flesh, in order that the righteous requirement of the law might be fulfilled in us, who walk not according to the flesh but according to the Spirit. For those who live according to the flesh set their minds on the things of the flesh, but those who live according to the Spirit set their minds on the things of the Spirit. For to set the mind on the flesh is death, but to set the mind on the Spirit is life and peace. For the mind that is set on the flesh is hostile to God, for it does not submit to God's law; indeed, it cannot. Those who are in the flesh cannot please God. Romans 8:1-8

We cannot be filled when we are living "according to the flesh," there is no authenticity in the flesh. True genuineness and authenticity come from the Spirit of God.

There is no condemnation or approval needed for those who live in Christ Jesus. When we walk in the Spirit, we are full of the Spirit because the law has been fulfilled in us. We must set our minds on God and what is truth. Live in the true authenticity God created for you. There is no condemnation or approval needed for those who are walking and living in the Spirit of Christ Jesus.

Journal

Day 7

Take time to meditate on God's word. What's on your heart this week?

_____

_____

_____

_____

_____

_____

_____

_____

_____

_____

_____

_____

_____

_____

_____

_____

_____

_____

Week Twenty-Six

Day 1

HOPE IN A REVOLVING WORLD

"He's got the whole world in His hands." Remember singing that song? "He's got the itty-bitty baby, He's got you and me brother, He's got you and me sister in His hands. He's got the whole world in His hands."

We are all brothers and sisters in Christ, and how true is this song? We are all in His hands, but how do you remain hopeful, positive, and focused when your world seems to be falling apart? The world keeps revolving even though sometimes ours seems to be crashing in. The hope we find in our revolving world is whose hands are revolving it. The One who made the galaxies is the same One who numbered the hairs on our head. God, our creator's hands are revolving our world no matter what we face, and we can remain hopeful in knowing that He has set His beautiful will in motion for our lives.

"When you pass through the waters, I will be with you; and when you pass through the rivers, they will not sweep over you. When you walk through the fire, you will not be burned; the flames will not set you ablaze." Isaiah 43:2 (NIV)

He never leaves us. He is always with us through each walk we take in life. Sometimes He will walk hand in hand. He will lead us or even carry us, but there will never be a time that He isn't there. Even in the fire of life, He will not let us be set ablaze.

Find hope and encouragement today in whose hands your world is revolving!

Day 2

OUR CONSTANT

Change. A lot of us are creatures of habit. We like for things to stay the same, but we all go through change. With life comes death. With day comes night. From the beginning of time, the earth and God's creations on earth have been ever-so-changing.

"You, Lord, laid the foundation of the earth in the beginning, and the heavens are the work of your hands; they will perish, but you remain; they will all wear out like a garment, like a robe you will roll them up, like a garment they will be changed. But you are the same, and your years will have no end." Hebrews 1:10-12

Our lives may continue to change, and all things may disappear, yet God's years have no end. His love and His faithfulness always remain the same. He will always be Yahweh. He laid the foundations of earth and the foundations of our lives. From the beginning until the end, as our lives shift, God will remain the same yesterday, today, and tomorrow.

Our foundations have been laid, and now we are to build them around the constant in our lives. God is the beginning and the end.

Day 3

WE ARE FAVORED

What does God say about us?

Even before he made the world, God loved us and chose us in Christ to be holy and without fault in his eyes.
Ephesians 1:4 (NLT)

1. He chose us.
2. We are holy.
3. We are unblemished.

We are not damaged. We are flawless, perfect, pure, and untouched. Do you believe that about yourself? That you are unblemished, without flaw? Or do you look in the mirror and see the blemishes, the hurt, the shame, the guilt, and the sin? God said that in His sight, in the sight of love, we are unblemished. We are perfect to Him. Those blemishes, the things you may see in the mirror, were washed clean. You are chosen. You are holy. You are blameless before God. He has made you all these things in the sight of His love and His image.

We need to see ourselves in the eyes of our Father and not in the eyes of the flesh or even in the eyes of others.

We are not damaged; we are favored!

Claim your blessing and fortune in God. You have been washed clean.

Day 4

LET HOPE GET AHOLD OF YOU

And hope does not put us to shame, because God's love has been poured into our hearts through the Holy Spirit who has been given to us. Romans 5:5

We all experience hope daily. We hope for good days, we hope our kids won't get into trouble, we hope we won't have anxiety attacks, we hope an illness will be cured, we even hope that we may be able to get home and relax.

The hope we have for certain things to happen is good motivation to know what God can do when He gets ahold of the things we worry about.

If we have hope in God, then worrying about those things coming to pass shouldn't be an issue.

Hope is a feeling in our hearts of something we strive for. We know our hope can be put to shame when our hope lies with God because he has poured it into us with His Holy Spirit. We are hopeful when we feel God moving, but when He is still, we worry about things He's already planning to take care of. God gives us hope so we are assured our desires have already been given to us.

For what have you stopped hoping? God wants you to recreate that hope in your heart that it will come to pass.

We should rejoice in hope; God knows our desires. He knows what's in and on our hearts. He knows more about us than we know about ourselves.

Hope deferred makes the heart sick, but a longing fulfilled is a tree of life. Proverbs 13:12

Don't lose hope in what God can do!

Be hopeful in today and joyful in tomorrow knowing He has already strategically planned your life just for you.

Day 5

GROWING IN OUR GOALS

I like to set goals. Whether they be long term or short term, I believe it's good to have goals for yourself and even for your family. Goals help you reach something that may seem unattainable at the time, but with effort and dedication become within reach.

Not that I have already obtained this or am already perfect, but I press on to make it my own, because Christ Jesus has made me his own. Brothers, I do not consider that I have made it my own. But one thing I do: forgetting what lies behind and straining forward to what lies ahead, I press on toward the goal for the prize of the upward call of God in Christ Jesus. Philippians 3:12-14

Paul speaks on His goal for the prize of the "upward call."

"But I PRESS ON…"

We keep moving forward toward the ultimate goal, which lives in Christ Jesus.

We will not be completely done in our walk until we meet Him face to face, but our long-term goal should be growing toward our upward call to be as much like Jesus as we can here on earth.

Day 6

REACH OUT

And behold, a woman who had suffered from a discharge of blood for twelve years came up behind him and touched the fringe of his garment, for she said to herself, "If only I touched his garment, I will be made well." Jesus turned and seeing her he said, "Take heart, daughter; your faith has made you well." And instantly the woman was made well.
Matthew 9:20-22

Would you reach out if you knew there was healing for your current situation?

This woman had a faith so big that even though she couldn't see the healing, she believed in it. For twelve years she had suffered, but she believed that if she reached out to Jesus and touched Him, she would be healed. We suffer through things and reach out to God, but sometimes I think instead of reaching out in faith we reach out in habit.

"God help me; God take this away," but do you believe what you are reaching for? Do you believe you are reaching into God's hands that are full of healing?

The key to having faith bigger than your situation is not in the norm, it's in believing and trusting in the supernatural.

Reach out today, not in habit but in faith. Know you are reaching for the healing!

Journal

Day 7

Take time to meditate on God's word. What's on your heart this week?

_____

_____

_____

_____

_____

_____

_____

_____

_____

_____

_____

_____

_____

_____

_____

_____

_____

_____

_____

Week Twenty-Seven

Day 1

YOU COULD BE THE PUZZLE PIECE

But God, who comforts the downcast, comforted us by the coming of Titus. 2 Corinthians 7:6

Paul says that Titus's arrival was all that he needed to get through a difficult time. It comforted him and reassured him of God's faithfulness.

We may be what someone else needs to help them get through a difficult time. Our words and faithfulness to God may be able to help them know they are not alone. There may be someone you can save today.

We need to grieve, but through God, not through the world.

For godly grief produces a repentance that leads to salvation without regret, whereas worldly grief produces death.
2 Corinthians 7:10

When Titus came, it reassured them of the love that God had for them. Titus was the piece they needed to know God was there. We may be the piece someone else needs to know God is still there. The reassurance that God is with them and has never left.

Don't allow others to experience worldly grief when you can step in and help them grieve in the presence of the Lord.

Be what others need.

Day 2

RIGHT WHERE THEY ARE

Ruth had a true loyalty to Naomi. Naomi was somewhat bitter from the things she had been through in life. She had gone through famine. She lost her husband and her sons. Naomi was left with her daughters-in-law but set off to go back to Bethlehem. She wanted her daughters-in-law to leave her and to just let her go by herself.

Have you ever been in that place, or do you know someone that is pushing everyone away? Sometimes it's loyalty that changes a person's mind. Sometimes we must go with others right where they are to show them that we aren't giving up or giving in. That's exactly what Ruth decided to do with Naomi.

And she said, "See, your sister in law has gone back to her people and to her gods; return after your sister in law." But Ruth said, "Do not urge me to leave you or to return from where you lodge I will lodge. Your people shall be my people, and your God my God. Where you die I will die, and there will I be buried. May the Lord do so to me and more also if anything but death parts me from you." And when Naomi saw that she was determined to go with her, she said no more.
Ruth 1:15-18

Sometimes we see things in others that they can't see in themselves. I think Ruth saw God in Naomi even when Naomi may not have been able to feel Him for herself because she had been harboring bitterness in her heart. Even though Naomi wasn't in a good place, it still shows how God was using her to also pursue and win Ruth's heart.

You never know when God is using you to help someone

else or vice versa. Loyalty and support could be all they need for a change of heart.

Walk with people where they are. God will pursue their heart but your loyalty to them may be where God is calling you to be.

Day 3

GOD IS ON THE RISE

God has called each of us accordingly. As I become closer to the Lord, I realize that the things happening around me, to myself and to others, are not always to be looked at as a bad thing. As much as God seems to be moving, the devil is around working overtime trying to steal the precious souls of those not planted firmly in their salvation. The only reason I can imagine the devil is working so hard is because he sees and knows God is on the rise.

But as for me, I will look to the Lord; I will wait for the God of my salvation; my God will hear me. Micah 7:7

It's easy for us all to get sidetracked from God. It's easy to stray, and it's easy to become engulfed by other things. It's becoming more of a reality that people are giving up on God and allowing the devil to step in, giving him opportunities to latch onto their lives in their thoughts and actions. Allowing them to become blinded to what God is trying to do for them and through them.

We can't give the devil any access! "We will wait for God; he is our salvation and he will hear us." God can teach us many things, but the one thing that comes to mind is patience. Sometimes God just wants us to look to Him and allow Him to work. For us to be still. As each year more and more kids and adults lose their lives to drugs and mental illness, it's apparent that the devil is creating these strongholds to kill, steal, and destroy. The enemy may be at work. But most importantly, that means God is RISING! We need our feet planted firmly or we too could fall so quickly. We need the armor of God!

Day 4

YOU ARE NOT FAULTY

We all face insecurities. We judge ourselves, find fault in who we are, and wish to be better or different. Wanting to better yourself for the Lord is a good thing, but critiquing who you are physically, mentally, and emotionally can be detrimental to our well-being. If we are not to judge others, why would we think judging ourselves is any better?

"Judge not, and you will not be judged; condemn not, and you will not be condemned; forgive, and you will be forgiven." Luke 6:37

God has placed each one of us here for a purpose. He uniquely made and molded each of us to his standards. We were not made to be compared. We do not need confirmation from others of who we are. We are children of God. He confirmed our existence and our purpose when He created us. Nothing or no one can take away what He has already proclaimed.

Don't allow feelings of insecurity and self-doubt to overwhelm and produce feelings of weakness. God does not create anything faulty. He has claimed each of us perfect in His eyes once we accepted Him into our hearts. Finding fault in what He made is allowing condemnation on yourself when only He can condemn.

Open your heart to love what He has created. We are all masterpieces in His eyes.

Day 5

BATTLE BETWEEN MIND & HEART

Life is full of adversity and trials. Satan can trick us into allowing fear, doubt, and worry to creep in, but God always has other plans. When God sees you overcome adversity, He sees growth, determination, and strength. He sees your heart is trusting in something better than yourself. He sees Himself in you.

With life comes tests, and with tests come failure and success. It's an ongoing battle of your mind and heart for what you're willing to give power to and what you're willing to rebuke and give no life to.

I think of Job and how he went through so much adversity, but even though the enemy struck him with many things, his heart belonged to God.

"Oh that my words were written! Oh that they were inscribed in a book! Oh that with an iron pen and lead they were engraved in the rock forever! For I know that my Redeemer lives, and that at the last he will stand upon the earth." Job 19:23-25

Our hearts, above all else, must be inscribed with God's love. We have to believe and know our redeemer is not dead, but He is alive inside of us.

He is alive, and He is inscribed in our hearts!

Day 6

HE SHUTS THE MOUTH

A lot of us have heard about Daniel and the lion's den. Daniel was thrown into the den, and at break of day the next day, the king went to see if "the God" that Daniel served had been able to deliver him from the mouths of the lions.

> *"O Daniel, servant of the living God, has your God, whom you serve continually, been able to deliver you from the lions?" Daniel 6:20*

Could you imagine the expression on his face when Daniel started to speak this next verse?

> *"'My God sent his angel and shut the lions' mouths, and they have not harmed me, because I was found blameless before him; and also before you.'" Daniel 6:22*

Well, that just happened. He sure did what I knew he would. He sent an angel and shut all their mouths. What?!

God does the same for us. He is always delivering us from those things we think are going "to be the death of us," and those who don't believe as we do are astonished. "What?! Your God did that?" "Yes, He did! My God did that, and guess what, He wants to be your God and do the same thing for you!" You are a walking testament of God's power. Share the news of what God has done for you today!

Journal

Day 7

Take time to meditate on God's word. What's on your heart this week?

_____

_____

_____

_____

_____

_____

_____

_____

_____

_____

_____

_____

_____

_____

_____

_____

_____

_____

Week Twenty-Eight

Day 1

FOUNTAIN OF LIFE

Sometimes you may hear people say that they want to drink from the fountain of youth and stay young forever. They don't ever want to get old. It's funny, when I was younger, I thought the same thing. Getting older meant something a lot different to me than it does now.

What if I told you we have a fountain of youth we can drink from or, better yet, a fountain of life?

For with you is the fountain of life; in your light do we see light.
Psalm 36:9

God is our fountain, and when we accept His son as our Savior, we drink from that fountain of everlasting life. The best thing is that His fountain never runs dry no matter how many people are drinking from it. We get to keep drinking and keep sharing it as much as we want. We choose how much life we feed into ourselves and how much our world is lit up by His light.

Only in His light can we see the light! Are you drinking from the fountain of life?

Day 2

FIND YOUR MOUNTAIN

And after he had dismissed the crowds, he went up on the mountain by himself to pray. When evening came, he was there alone, but the boat by this time was a long way from the land, beaten by the waves, for the wind was against them. Matthew 14:23-24

This was right before Jesus walked on water. He went up to a mountain to pray by himself. Prayer is such an important aspect of our lives. If the Savior of the world was practicing finding a spot and going in prayer alone, I would think we need to mimic His ways and do the same.

In these verses it doesn't say the time frame of how long He prayed or even what He prayed about. We just know that He prayed until evening, and by the time He came back to the boat, it had made its way out into the water. If we put all that together, I'm guessing that He was on the mountain quite a while.

We need a prayer life. If we think about all the time, we spend focused on communicating with those around us in our everyday lives; our families, coworkers, or friends and compare that to the little bit of time we spend communicating with God, we can see what our priorities are.

God longs to hear from us. Try to find your mountain today and spend some time with your Father in prayer.

Day 3

STUMBLING BLOCKS

As we walk with Christ, it's important for us to avoid the stumbling blocks and to not be a stumbling block for others. Each of our walks looks different. Some things can be right for you to do as a Christian, and some aren't so right for others.

We are the church. You and I may attend a physical church, but ultimately our bodies are the living church. We have to begin to view ourselves as that and walk in that as God would have us to do. When we think of ourselves in that manner you can see the importance of us not becoming a stumbling block for those around us.

For if your brother is grieved by what you eat, you are no longer walking in love. Romans 14:15

For the kingdom of God is not a matter of eating and drinking but of righteousness and peace and joy in the Holy Spirit. Whoever thus serves Christ is acceptable to God and approved by men. Romans 14: 17-18

We are not here to judge or condemn others for what they do for Christ. We are here to build them up. We must be conscious of our walk and the walks of fellow Christians around us. We need to make sure that we aren't pulling them into our walks and causing them to stumble and fall away from what God is calling them to do. We should want everyone to walk in faith being the church everywhere they go.

Day 4

MERCY & GRACE

Who do we usually invite over for dinner or decide to have dinner with? They are usually those who are close to us or have something in common with us. Those we want to get to know more. I love in Matthew when it says,

And as Jesus reclined at table in the house, behold, many tax collectors and sinners came and were reclining with Jesus and his disciples.
Matthew 9:10

When you recline, you lie back somewhere on a couch, in a chair, or wherever you need to feel comfortable. If Jesus was reclining, to me it means that He must have felt comfortable at the table with these sinners and tax collectors.   If Jesus was uncomfortable and showed it through His posture, these people would have been able to tell, but instead, Jesus wanted to get to know them more.

And when the Pharisees saw this, they said to his disciples, "Why does your teacher eat with tax collectors and sinners?" But when He heard it, he said, "Those who are well have no need of a physician, but those who are sick. Go and learn what this means: 'I desire mercy, and not sacrifice. For I came not to call the righteous, but sinners.'"
Matthew 9:11-13

He desires for us to show mercy. I think He shows us here that the mercy He desires is to be for everyone, even those who we know are doing wrong. He wants us to show mercy and grace to everyone. He didn't come to call those who were already believers, He came to save those who were sinners. That's what He wants us to do. He gave us a calling and a job to save those that don't know Him. To

recline at the table with someone and lead them to Him. Let's make sure we are reclining and making ourselves comfortable for what He has shown us to do.

Day 5

VOICE OF GREAT MULTITUDE

Can you imagine when the heavens roar and shout praises? The way they sing, how their voices harmonize and are in perfect unison? How loud and beautiful it is?

After the fall of Babylon, we see how we should rejoice.

Then I heard what seemed to be the voice of a great multitude, like a roar of many waters and like the sound of mighty peals of thunder, crying out, "Hallelujah! For the Lord our God the almighty reigns."
Revelations 19:6

I don't know about you, but I want to praise my God with a voice like the roar of waters and the sound of thunder.

I want to praise Him before, during, and after the storm. I want to learn to praise Him crying out, "Hallelujah," and always remembering He is the King of Kings and Lord of Lords. He is our God Almighty.

Praise God today, shout His name, and lift your hands. Our God reigns.

He is the ruler of the nations and the King of our lives.

He lives forever. Make a roar like thunder today, and praise His name singing Hallelujah!

Day 6

FULL FORCE

God's love for us is so much bigger than the mistakes we've made.

A lot of people think that because they've done things that God would frown upon, they are unworthy of His love and mercy. That can't be any further from the truth. We all sin, we all make mistakes, but those are the times when God wants us to call out for His love the most.

"Before I formed you in the womb I knew you, and before you were born I consecrated you; I appointed you a prophet to the nations."
Jeremiah 1:5

He knew our trials, our tribulations, our successes, and our failures all before we even understood the glory He would bring into our lives. No one is perfect, we all fall short, but because of His love for us we can ask for forgiveness in those times and move forward. We were created by Him to be loved by Him.

"You are not an accident. There are accidental parents, but there are no accidental births. There are illegitimate parents, but there are no illegitimate children. There are unplanned pregnancies, but there are no un-purposed people. God wanted you in this world. You are not an accident."
-WHAT ON EARTH AM I HERE FOR, by Rick Warren

God wants you to come as you are. If you're broken, if you're lost, if you're questioning your faith in Him, He still wants all of you. He wants you to give Him your all so that He can move mountains in your life. He wants all your

mistakes, all your troubles, and all your fears. He wants to show you how, when giving Him the glory and living your life completely and truly for Him, He can remove all those doubts and troubles and give you peace. God wants you to come to Him full force.

It's in Christ that we find out who we are and what we are living for... Ephesians 1:11-12(MSG)

Life is a constant battle. There is so much destruction and hurt in this world. People are always questioning what is true. Go to God, follow Him, seek His love. He wants you just as you are because you were created for so much more.

Journal

Day 7

Take time to meditate on God's word. What's on your heart this week?

_____

_____

_____

_____

_____

_____

_____

_____

_____

_____

_____

_____

_____

_____

_____

_____

_____

_____

_____

Week Twenty-Nine

Day 1

IN DEPTH JEALOUSY

Everyone has been jealous of something. It could be that your friend's ice cream flavor they picked out looks better than the one you picked, or it could be a deeper jealousy.

God is jealous for us. The jealousy that God experiences for us must be just as heart wrenching or more so than the jealousy we experience here on earth. The difference is that our jealousy is critical, harmful, and detrimental to where God wants us. Those feelings can keep us from God himself. God's jealousy is meaningful and predestined for what He wants for our lives.

Have you been or are you jealous? We need to direct our jealousy to the one who is jealous for us. Let's begin to be jealous for our relationship with our Father, being protective over it and defined in it.

Wrath is cruel, anger is overwhelming, but who can stand before jealousy? Proverbs 27:4

The only one who can stand before jealousy is our God. Let Him stand in for you.

Day 2

GO TELL

A voice says, "Cry!"
And I said, "What shall I cry?"

All flesh is grass, and all its beauty is like the flower of the field. The grass withers, the flower fades when the breath of the Lord blows on it; surely the people are grass. The grass withers, the flower fades, but the word of our God will stand forever. Isaiah 40:6-8

Ever wondered what God wants you to do? "What do I cry out, Lord? What do I tell others about you, and how do I do it?"

Here, the Lord says, "Cry," which means go tell, go preach, and let the world know the truth. Isaiah says in this instance exactly what we say sometimes, "What shall I cry?"

The Lord just wants us to cry out the truth. He wants us to tell about the one thing that will never change. He knows all things will fade and wither away. The grass withers, and the flowers fade, but there will always be one thing that remains the same.

Our flesh is weak, and our beauty will grow dim, but there is something that will stay the same forever, and that is the word of God.

So, go tell, go cry out to everyone what is honorable and true. Open your Bible and read what will never change. God's word is firmly planted and will continue to be for years to come. It will stand forever!

Day 3

THE CROSS

For me, the cross is always a reminder of God's love for us. It's also a reminder of the sacrifice Jesus made to take away our sins so that we can have eternal life.

The cross was a platform where God told His Son He must go to save people like you and me. He carried the cross (He carries our sins), so that we sinners could be free from the sins of the world when we accept Him as our Lord and Savior.

When I see the cross, I also see power. God's great power over you and me.

For the wages of sin is death, but the gift of God is eternal life through Jesus Christ our Lord. Romans 6:23

Can you see and feel God's power?

For the wages of sin is death.....

Though we are all sinners, the cross is a reminder that even though God knew we would sin, He also knew His great love for us was more powerful than any sin we could ever commit. The cross says, "I still love you even though you sin."

Jesus died on the cross for all of us sinners, so that when we go to the cross, we can be lifted from our sins and be made new in Him. The cross is not where love ended, but to me, the cross is where my love started. The day that Jesus was

called by our Father to be crucified on the cross so that I could be set free from this world and one day live with Him, is by far beyond any love I can fathom. Even though I may not be able to come close to understanding that kind of love, I am still able to see that love from Him daily through what He continues to do in my life.

God knew His Son would die that day for us, but He also knew that on the third day He would rise again because nothing can hold down the power of God!

Day 4

THE GREAT I AM

Knock Knock
Who's there?
It's Me God.
God who?

I used to love joke books growing up. Those or mad libs to fill out. Those were the things I wanted when we were taking long road trips. I'd read them to my family and fill in the blanks.

God isn't a knock knock joke, but do you know how many people around us are continuing to knock at all kinds of other doors besides His? We are the ones who need to be saying, "Let me tell you what happens when you choose to knock at His door. His door will never close, it is ever revolving. His door always says welcome. Once you enter His door you will become changed."

Knock Knock
Who's there?
It's I Am.
I Am who?

The God, I Am. Your Father, God. God of love, God who is spirit and truth. I Am is the King of Kings, the Lord of Lords.

"I am the Alpha and the Omega, the first and the last, the beginning and the end." Revelations 22:13

Let's help lead others to the door that opens many blessings.

God's door. The Great I Am. This door is always open, and they don't even have to knock. God's just waiting for them to enter. Let's tell others about the great I Am today. We carry disappointment, just as we carry shame, hurt and many other feelings. People and things disappoint us daily, but God never disappoints.

Day 5

GOD SAYS WATCH ME

I started thinking about Sarah (Sarai) in the Bible. How disappointed she must have felt for years not being able to carry a child. The disappointment she felt as a wife. Then as if that wasn't enough, the disappointment she felt when Hagar was able to carry Abraham's child. She was disappointed repeatedly, until God finally came and spoke to both her and Abraham.

"I will bless her, and moreover, I will give you a son by her. I will bless her, and she shall become nations; kings of people shall come from her." Genesis 17:16

God speaks with Abraham and tells him Sarah will have his child, but think about how many years have gone by, and she hasn't been able to get pregnant. Abraham is now 99 and Sarah 90.

Now read this.

Now Abraham and Sarah were old, advanced in years. The way of women had ceased to be with Sarah. So Sarah laughed to herself, saying, "After I am worn out, and my lord is old, shall I have pleasure?" The Lord said to Abraham, "Why did Sarah laugh and say, 'Shall I indeed bear a child, now that I am old?' Is anything too hard for the Lord? At the appointed time I will return to you, about this time next year, and Sarah shall have a son." But Sarah denied it, saying, "I did not laugh," for she was afraid. He said, "No, but you did laugh." Genesis 18:11-15

God calls her out for not believing what He can do. What's He calling you out for right now that you aren't believing?

"Is anything too hard for the Lord?" What are you disappointed about? You've been praying for it and it hasn't happened. What have you kind of said, "Yeah, right" to?

God says, "Watch me!"

Day 6

SIN IS DEAD

Jesus died so that we could live. When we think of death, we don't think of life. When we think of death, we think of sadness, grief, and sorrow. When we think of death as our life through Christ, it means something different. The death of Christ on the cross means we have come alive.

For the death he died he died to sin, once for all, but the life he lives he lives to God. So you also must consider yourselves dead to sin and alive to God in Christ Jesus.
Romans 6:10-11

Jesus died for our sin, and as the scripture says, "ONCE FOR ALL." "Once for all" means the sin is no longer, and it was for everyone. No matter the sin. No matter the decision. No matter how many years have passed. He died for all. When it comes to sin, though, we too must consider ourselves dead to it. If Jesus died for it, the sin in us died that day as well. When Jesus took up the cross, He killed our sins.

That means the sin you are gripped in that you committed years ago is dead!

We are alive, but we are not alive living in past or future sin. We are alive living for God in Jesus Christ knowing our past sin and sin to come is dead.

Journal

Day 7

Take time to meditate on God's word. What's on your heart this week?

_____

_____

_____

_____

_____

_____

_____

_____

_____

_____

_____

_____

_____

_____

_____

_____

_____

_____

_____

_____

_____

Week Thirty

Day 1

SOUL CHECK

Bitter has two different meanings: one is an unpleasant taste and the other is feelings of anger, hurt, or resentment. Either way, they kind of work together because if you're bitter about someone or something you've probably allowed a "bad taste" to be put into your mouth.

I have found that what we feed ourselves is truly what gives life to our hearts and minds. Not just food, but thoughts with which we are feeding our minds. If you're constantly reminding yourself of all the bad things that have happened, then that's what's going to consume your mind. If you're dwelling on what someone has or hasn't done to you, then those are the thoughts that makes that bitter taste begin to form.

Naomi was bitter. She was bitter that she had lost everything: her sons, her husband, where she lived, and even all her food. She became so bitter and continued to feed those thoughts to herself for so long that she even begins to feed them to others.

She said to them, "Do not call me Naomi; call me Mara (which means bitter) for the almighty has dealt very bitterly with me. I went away full, and the Lord has brought me back empty. Why call me Naomi, when the Lord has testified against me and the almighty has brought calamity upon me?" Ruth 1:20-21

Naomi isn't just bitter but is now throwing that bitterness and those lies she has started to believe on those around her. We have to be careful about what we are allowing to

consume us because eventually those same things can begin to consume those around us.

Could someone call you Mara? Are you walking around with a "bad taste" believing lies and feeding yourself with the wrong things? Today I'd like to call a "soul check." Check what you're allowing to consume you.

Day 2

GO TO BATLE

A lot of us know about the story of David and Goliath. Where David, who tends sheep, ends up being the one who strikes down the big giant Goliath. David was the underdog, the one no one would have chosen to go to battle. Nevertheless, with just a sling and a stone, we see that David comes out on top. That he prevails to everyone's surprise.

We all face many battles in life. Maybe not having to go to literal war, but we may be in spiritual warfare - war in our minds, with our families, coworkers, even in a sickness. The enemy always wants us to feel like we are in battle and we are at war. I'm here to tell you that no matter what war you may face today or in the future, you've got someone bigger going up to battle for you. It may seem like you're the underdog in your situation, but the battle isn't truly yours. Just as the battle wasn't truly David's.

"and that all this assembly may know that the Lord saves not with sword and spear. For the battle is the Lord's, and he will give you into our hand." 1 Samuel 17:47

The battle is the Lord's. If the battle is His, then it's not what we can do, it's what He can do through us. Do you seem unequipped for the battle you're up against?

I'm sure David felt the same way with just a sling and a stone. What we must realize is that when our sight is on the Lord, no matter what we may have, we aren't in lack with Him. Be confident in Christ against whatever battle you may be up against. "For the battle is the Lord's."

Day 3

HE HOLDS THE POWER

He gives strength to the weary and increases the power of the weak.
Isaiah 40:29 (NIV)

Finally, be strong in the Lord and in his mighty power.
Ephesians 6:10

God's power can't really be described in words. His power is so intense, so strong that there really isn't just one word that could give it a perfectly accurate description.

Nothing has power without God. All those things that seem like they are burdening you have no power without God. Nothing can be shaken, and nothing can be broken without the power of God. You may give your worry, addiction, fear, and defeat power, but your power loses all credit without God's name in it.

If you don't have God's power over you, you have nothing. His name is the only name that should hold power over us. Nothing has any power to stand against us unless it was formed within Him. God holds all the power!

"But in that coming day no weapon turned against you will succeed. You will silence every voice raised up to accuse you. These benefits are enjoyed by the servants of the Lord." Isaiah 54:17 (NLT)

Nothing formed against us can stand when we live in God's power. Believe that today.

Day 4

RUN THE RACE

I'm not a runner. I can run, but it's not something I would choose to just go outside and do. On the other hand, some love doing it. It's a way to clear their minds while doing something they enjoy.

We are all running a race for God. How are you running your race?

Do you not know in a race all the runners run, but only one receives the prize? So run so that you may obtain it. Every athlete exercises self-control in all things. They do it to receive a perishable wreath, but we an imperishable.
1 Corinthians 9:24-25

We aren't in a race with others when it comes to our faith, but we are in a constant race with ourselves. We are racing in our minds every day. We are constantly having to build our endurance through seeking God. We must continue to build ourselves just as a runner would build their endurance for their race. We must keep our eyes on the prize - our eternal life in heaven with Him.

It's easy to get tired and want to give up. It was never promised to be an easy race, but it's worth the prize we will obtain at the end.

Practice exercising self-control today. We are all athletes for God!

Day 5

GIFT OF WORSHIP

Therefore let us be grateful for receiving a kingdom that cannot be shaken, and thus let us offer to God acceptable worship, with reverence and awe, for our God is a consuming fire. Hebrews 12:28-29

This verse tells us how to serve God with adoration. If God answered none of our prayers, and if He stopped moving, do we truly realize that what He has already done is more than enough? I'm totally guilty of needing more. We all need Him and want Him to still answer prayers and come through in areas of our lives, but truly if He never did anything else, He has already done more than enough. This verse shows us His promise. He has provided us with a kingdom in heaven that cannot and will not be shaken. This verse also tells us that we are to offer Him something. Instead of thinking of the things He will and can continue to offer us, this verse tells us what we can offer Him.

God wants us to present a gift to Him. He has given us all many gifts, but this is something that anyone and everyone can do. We are to present Him with the gift of worship. I believe this is a powerful way of deep communication with God. It allows His consuming fire to be ignited inside of us. It says we should worship with reverence, which means we are to show deep respect when we worship. This shows Him our hearts and humbles us. If He does nothing else, He has already done enough. He is enough.

Today, I think we should worship in a new light with even more respect for our Father. Worship Him, not expecting anything or asking for anything but know that we have already received more than enough through Him.

Day 6

HE GOES ALONGSIDE US

When we are doing things with the Lord, we are doing things with purpose. When we choose to do things without Him those things are pointless, useless, and done in vain.

Unless the Lord builds the house, those who build it labor in vain. Unless the Lord watches over the city, the watchman stays awake in vain. It is in vain that you rise up early and go late to rest, eating the bread of anxious toil; for he gives to his beloved sleep. Psalm 127:1-2

We must invite God alongside us in whatever we do - in parenting, in our relationships, in our health, when we go to work, new journeys we want to embark on, and the list can go on. When God is with us, we cannot fail. Where He is, so is His hand in what we are doing.

When God is in participation there will always be a favorable outcome. There will always be success.

We must invite God into our daily lives. When we are doing things with and for the Lord, we can expect His results. Sometimes, if we don't feel Him, it could be because of something as simple as we haven't asked Him to come into our situation. God wants our acknowledgement.

Is there something you are dealing with today in which you feel a lack of God's presence? God hasn't gone anywhere, but maybe you have. Take time today to ask Him to come in and take over. Ask for His hand on your situation and wait for the blessings. They will come

Journal

Day 7

Take time to meditate on God's word. What's on your heart this week?

_____

_____

_____

_____

_____

_____

_____

_____

_____

_____

_____

_____

_____

_____

_____

_____

_____

_____

_____

Week Thirty-One

Day 1

DEALT A BAD HAND

You can find some of Joseph's story in Genesis 37:18-36. Joseph's brothers wanted to kill him, but instead, they decided to sell him into slavery. One brother later went and tried to save Joseph but realized he was gone. The story goes on to say that Joseph was given to a king, and after being thrown into jail for being wrongly accused, the king later realized that they could benefit from Joseph and his abilities. Joseph ended up overseeing all the land in Egypt, and later, his brothers ended up bowing down to him.

Some would say that Joseph was dealt some bad hands. His brothers hated him, he was sold into slavery, and thrown into jail for something he didn't do; but God knew His plans for Joseph.

You may be going through something now that seems unfair, draining, and scary; but just as God had other plans for Joseph, He has the same for you. He has already called you His. God wants you to trust Him where you are.

God will not forsake us nor leave us.

*And those who know your name put their trust in you, for you, O
Lord, have never forsaken those who seek you.
Psalm 9:10*

Through your situation there will be light. God wants us to believe in His power and His capabilities and not our own. He wants us to rely on him, trusting the process for His bigger plan for our life. Sometimes our own plans are not

what God has designed. God has a far better plan for us, and we must trust Him in getting us there.

God has equipped us to handle each situation and circumstance. He has prepared us for each battle with what we need, knowing that if we put all our trust in Him, we will be triumphant because He has already claimed the victory over the situation.

Trust in the Lord with all your heart and lean not on your own understanding; in all your ways submit to him, and he will make your paths straight.
Proverbs 3:5-7 (NIV)

Day 2

WORD OF GOD

As he said these things, a woman in the crowd raised her voice and said to him, "Blessed is the womb that bore you, and the breasts at which you nursed!" But He said, "Blessed rather are those who hear the word of God and keep it!" Luke 11:27-28

I can't imagine the happiness that having the Son of God brought to Mary's life. What she must have felt being the mother of the Savior of the world. Jesus knew Mary was blessed, but He also knew that the blessing didn't come from her bearing Him. The true blessing didn't come from the act of her carrying Him. The true blessing comes from the decision that everyone gets to choose. It was decided that Mary would carry our Savior, but it's decided by us if we will receive our Savior and the word of the Lord.

It's our choice to put what we hear and read into use in our lives.

The greatest blessing that we can ever obtain is obeying what the word of God says.

Jesus says to hear it and keep it. The word of God is the most precious gift.

Day 3

TAKE HEART

When offense comes your way, what do you do with it? Are you now or have you been offended by something someone has done, and you think about it occasionally? In Matthew, the Pharisees were offended by something the disciples said.

And he called the people to him and said to them, "Hear and understand: it is not what goes into the mouth that defiles a person, but what comes out of the mouth; this defiles a person." Then the disciples came and said to him, "Do you know that the Pharisees were offended when they heard this saying?" Matthew 15:10-12

I think this verse teaches us a lot. When we are offended, I think we have to take heart. If you read a little further down in the scripture, you will see that it says what's in your heart is what defines you.

"But what comes out of the mouth proceeds from the heart, and this defiles a person." Matthew 15:18

Offense is something that is going to come. What we do with the offense is what defines our hearts. Therefore, I say we have to be ready to "TAKE HEART." We must constantly clean out what's in our hearts. Making sure that offense doesn't take root. What we allow to take up room inside our hearts is important, and offense has no room. If we allow the offense to have room inside our hearts, then it will start to be what comes out of our mouths. To me, "taking heart" means protecting what I allow inside of it. Are we not cautious of what we allow to go inside the people's hearts that we love the most - our spouse, our kids,

our close family and friends? If you can't answer "yes" to that, then maybe it's time to start taking out the trash that is inside of yours. Be cautious of what you allow inside your heart because it can be what comes out of your mouth and then take root inside someone else.

Day 4

YOKE OF SLAVERY

Freedom: the state of being free or at liberty rather than in confinement or under physical restraint.

Do you realize that for us the cross should represent freedom? We begin to forget what the meaning of freedom is, and who it truly comes from. Sometimes we may even look for freedom in things of this world.

Freedom is something that Jesus gave us on the cross so that we could surrender anything and everything that imprisons us - all those thoughts that hold us captive and keep us from knowing what God says is true.

For I know the plans I have for you, declares the Lord, plans for welfare and not for evil, to give you a future and a hope.
Jeremiah 29:11

It is for freedom that Christ has set us free. Stand firm, then, and do not let yourselves be burdened again by a yoke of slavery.
Galatians 5:1 (NIV)

Freedom was already given to us, and it has set us free. We can't allow ourselves to fall back into the yoke of slavery. The "yoke of slavery" could be worry, fear, doubt, jealousy, envy, and the list could go on. What's your yoke of slavery?

Today, think about the things that hold you back from feeling the true freedom that Jesus Christ gave you on the cross. Begin to stand firm on the promises and break the chains that are binding you. God wants you to live a life in full freedom, starting today!

Day 5

THE REFELECTION OF HIM

Have you ever caught the reflection of something out of the corner of your eye and had to do a double take to make sure it was what you saw?

Lord, was that a sign? Did you just send me a sweet reminder?

I want to make sure that I'm catching those reflections, and that I'm also in tune with my own.

Our own reflections may not be reflecting His character. We often get carried away in our own messes, and we fail to insert God into them. The busyness of life causes us to pass right by those sweet reflections of Him.

He is all around us.

This morning don't pass by the sweet reflection of Him as you look in the mirror. He is inside of you. Today as you look in the mirror at the reflection of you, who was made in His image, remind yourself of this scripture.

"Fear not, for I have redeemed you; I have called you by name, you are mine." Isaiah 43:1

Let this be a reminder as we look at ourselves this morning that we are His and He is ours. The reflection of you reflects the Him inside of you. Take His reflection with you today and stand confidently in it.

Day 6

MAKING A WAY

Has God ever made a way for you, or are you currently waiting and praying for Him to make a way?

As we were teaching the little kids one day about Moses parting the red sea, all I could think about was how God is always clearing paths in our own lives and making ways for us where we may see no way.

The Egyptians were after the people of Israel, and the people of Israel feared what would happen if they got to them. They cried out saying, "Why did you bring us out of there for them to chase us down and kill us? It would have been better if we would have just stayed and served them."

And Moses said to the people, "Fear not, stand firm, and see the salvation of the Lord, which he will work for you today. For the Egyptians whom you see today, you shall never see again. The Lord will fight for you, and you have only to be silent." Exodus 14:13-14

What's your "Egyptian" that's chasing after you or fighting you today? God says to fear not and stand firm. See the salvation of your Lord through this. Don't be scared. God is on your side, and whatever God needs to "part," He will for you just as He did for Moses and the people of Israel.

Then Moses stretched out his hand over the sea, and the Lord drove the sea back by a strong east wind all night and made the sea dry land, and the waters were divided.
Exodus 14:21

He allowed Moses and the people of Israel to pass through,

but they were still being chased. God then told Moses to raise his staff again, and the sea would go back to normal while the Egyptians were still in the middle of crossing it.

I believe sometimes our staffs can be our very hands God gave us - raising them to Him and asking God to help us or laying them on others and asking God to help them.

The Lord will deliver you just as He delivered Moses and the people of Israel. Raise your hands today against whatever you're fighting or facing. Fear not and stand firm.

"The Lord will fight for you." Exodus 14:14

Journal

Day 7

Take time to meditate on God's word. What's on your heart this week?

_____

_____

_____

_____

_____

_____

_____

_____

_____

_____

_____

_____

_____

_____

_____

_____

_____

_____

_____

_____

_____

Week Thirty-Two

Day 1

IT TAKES TIME

Paul was called by God to go preach His word to the people in Syria and Cilicia. They didn't know Paul, but they had heard who he was, someone who used to practice Judaism and persecuted the church of God.

But when he who had set me apart before I was born, and who had called me by his grace, was pleased to reveal his son to me, in order that I might preach him among the Gentiles, I did not immediately consult with anyone.
Galatians 1:15-16

Paul was not living for God, but God saw something in Paul, just as He sees something in us no matter where we are or what we have done. God still saw something in Paul and chose Him to share His word.

Paul says he didn't immediately consult with anyone. He went away for three years. Sometimes it takes time, and that's okay. When Paul came back from those three years, He started to preach His faith, and many people glorified God because of him.

God has called us all no matter what we've done or where we've been. God can use you! God has chosen you to do His mighty works.

Day 2

GRIEVING HOLDS
ITS OWN EXPLAINATION

Mourning is unexplainable pain. We can explain our happiness. We can even explain our anger or sadness, but grief holds its own explanation. It may be evident why we are grieving, but at times, the actual process through the pain can't be described. It's a deep wound that's valid, raw, and open. It's a hurt that surpasses all fleshly understanding. It can truly bring no words. Mourning and grief can put us in an emotional state that causes a lot of deep feelings to arise. Mourning can be overwhelming, fear bound, breathtaking, and mind tackling. It's painful, messy, and gut wrenching.

What helps us get through these dark, deep emotions? Hope.

Faith in someone and something bigger than all the words just written down.

GOD. God binds our wounds.

He heals the brokenhearted and binds up their wounds.
Psalm 147:3

He never leaves us through the process.

The Lord is close to the brokenhearted and saves those who are crushed
in spirit. Psalm 34:18 (NIV)

We are promised that this is not our forever and that one

day there will be no more death. He cares for and wipes away each individual tear as they fall.

"He will wipe away every tear from their eyes. There will be no more death' or mourning or crying or pain, for the old order of things has passed away."
Revelation 21:4 (NIV)

We have to learn how to lean on God and not our own understanding through these times. We can have hope, faith, and God right beside us holding our hands as we walk through, and we can rest in all the promises He has made to us.

Day 3

WORTHY ENOUGH

What if God critiqued us as we critique ourselves at times?! We are all usually our own worst critic. Whether it's finding fault in the way we look, or how we do something. We pick ourselves apart little by little until we begin to believe what we've trained our minds to think. We aren't good enough. We can't get anything right. Why can't I be more like so-and-so; they seem like they have it all together? The negative thoughts begin to consume us, and before we know it, we are wanting to change something about our inward or outward appearance.

Thank goodness we serve a God who doesn't critique us for everything we think we do wrong or can't get right. Our God loves us for who we are, not for what we've done or not done. Jesus died to take away all those things on the cross. He loves us just the way He created us. He sees our hearts and the beauty inside of them.

God is here to bring us back when we think we fall short. He is there to love us when we can't find the love to love ourselves. God isn't here to condemn us, so we need to stop condemning ourselves. We are more than what we see; we are worthy. God called us worthy the day He sent his Son to die on the cross for us. If we are worthy in His eyes, we should be worthy in our own.

Therefore, there is now no condemnation for those who are in Christ Jesus. Romans 8:1 (NIV)

Day 4

NO CONTINGENCIES

Have you ever thought about what a conditional world we live in? A lot of times people won't do anything for others unless they are getting something in return. If you scratch my back, I'll scratch yours. Let's be honest. There are times at night my husband wants me to scratch his head, and I may say something like, "Okay, I'll do it for 15 minutes, but then you have to play with my hair for 15 minutes."

We live in a world where we can do something for someone, but only in return for us getting something back from them. Is giving really giving if we do it with a selfish heart? I can even remember a time when I gave a contingency to God, "God if you do this in my life, I won't ever do this again." Can you imagine what God thinks when we give Him conditions? Honestly, I can imagine Him laughing and thinking, "Oh child, you really don't grasp My love for you."

What's love if there is contingency? We should do the right thing, the nice thing, help someone, or love on someone, not needing anything in return. I'm glad that everything I have ever gone to God in prayer for He hasn't put conditions on based on what I was doing for Him. We serve a God that does things without contingencies. He does all things just because He loves us. There is no reason besides love. Let's live less in contingencies and more in "JUST BECAUSE."

Let all that you do be done in love.
1 Corinthians 16:14

Day 5

SERVE & BE SERVED

One thing I have learned is that in order to serve we also have to be willing to be served. God wants us to be humble in Him, and in order to do that, we also have to humbly accept other servants of God to serve us wherever we are.

Serving God is much more than just on a Sunday. Serving God is opening our hearts to our everyday lives to figure out where we can be used whenever He needs us. Personally, I like to see where God is directing me to serve Him. Trying to be in tune with who is put in my path to touch and serve as He would. Whether it's the urge to speak to someone I have never met or trying to put a smile on the face of the person running the drive thru. It could be simply reaching out to someone I haven't heard from in a while. Serving God isn't supposed to be hard, and it's not meant to feel like a job. When we serve, we are supposed to do it with happy and content hearts. We were meant to serve others, just as others were meant to serve us. Life wasn't meant to be done alone or not to be done with grateful hearts.

Use today to serve in any capacity. If you see someone drop something, pick it up for them with a smile. If you see someone in need, pray with them. Gladness in serving will reflect the servant's heart. If it's you in need, allow that other person to serve you no matter how big or small.

Serve the Lord with gladness!
Psalm 100:2

Day 6

FEELING JUSTIFICATIONS

Feelings, don't we all have them? I don't know about you, but I may have a little too many at times. I'm talking about the good feelings and the bad ones. We can't just always have those good ones, we have those bad ones, too.

I'm thankful for my openness to feel, but if we aren't careful, those feelings can put us in a whirlwind of other things causing strife inside of us, right?

Aren't you glad that our relationships with Christ aren't based off a feeling?

I was reminded one night after an event that every time you expect to get those feel-goods, it's okay if you don't.

God doesn't want our feelings to justify our actions. He wants our actions to justify our feelings.

Our action is that we love Him and that our love abides in Him; our feelings are always concrete in our Savior.

When we are missing that feel-good, it may be because we've missed the purpose of what He has come to do. God has given us the ability to feel both good and bad, but what are we doing with those feelings?

Take action on your feelings today!

"For to set the mind on the flesh is death, but to set the mind on the Spirit is life and peace." Romans 8:6

Journal

Day 7

Take time to meditate on God's word. What's on your heart this week?

_____

_____

_____

_____

_____

_____

_____

_____

_____

_____

_____

_____

_____

_____

_____

_____

_____

_____

_____

_____

Week Thirty-Three

Day 1

HE IS STRONG

I am thankful to serve a God who's bigger than my struggles. In those times where the weight feels too much for us to carry, we must begin to let go and let Him take over. God is our stronghold. He is there when we are weak, fragile, and hurt. He gives us the opportunity to allow Him to carry our burdens. The weight of our burdens should not drag us down if we have faith in a God who is bigger than our struggles.

But he said to me, "My grace is sufficient for you, for my power is made perfect in weakness." Therefore I will boast all the more gladly of my weaknesses, so that the power of Christ may rest upon me.
2 Corinthians 12:9

Who doesn't want the power of Christ to rest upon them? His power in our weakness is more substantial than anything we can do. His power is where our weaknesses are made perfect.

For the sake of Christ, then, I am content with weaknesses, insults, hardships, persecutions, and calamities. For when I am weak, then I am strong. 2 Corinthians 12:10

When we are weak, our strength is found in Him alone. We can be content in our struggle because God is bigger than our fears. God's hand is on our situation. Everything can be made perfect within Him. In flooded fields, plants still grow roots. When we are in a flooded time, that's when our roots can grow the strongest for God. Allow your roots to grow and see what God can do,

Day 2

PREPARE YOUR HEART

Can you think of a time when you were walking without God? Maybe it's now, or maybe it was years ago. I can remember a time in my life when I felt like my walk wasn't anything other than "my" walk. I remember how hard of a walk that was.

When we walk with God, life is just a lot easier. There are still trials and tribulations, but life isn't as hard to handle when we have someone already fighting things for us before we even arrive in them. God gives us the wisdom to know what to do. He gives us the opportunity to make our own choices and to decide whether to draw near to Him. We can only become wise in God when we fear His capabilities.

Who is wise and understanding among you? Let them show it by their good life, by deeds done in humility that comes from wisdom.
James 3:13 (NIV)

God gives us the wisdom to get through and to get over. He supplies us with the understanding we need; we must be willing to gain what we need from Him to draw us closer to Him.

We can't become wise in our ways without preparing our hearts.

Day 3

WE ARE NO CONTENDER

"Shall a faultfinder contend with the Almighty? He who argues with God, let him answer it." Job 40:2

To be sure, in all our lives we have found fault with something or someone. Have you ever tried to contend with God? If I'm being honest with myself, there have been times that I have felt like I was trying to go to battle with Him. I disagreed with everything that was going on in my life, and quite frankly, I wondered why in the world He thought it was a good idea.

We all find fault with where we are as Job did in these moments when he had everything stripped from him. Even with everything stripped from us, we are nothing in comparison to the battle God is standing in fighting for us. In the next verse, Job answers the Lord and says,

"Behold I am a small account: what shall I answer you? I lay my hand on my mouth. I have spoken once, and I will not answer; twice, but I will proceed no further." Job 40:4-5

These verses made me stop in my tracks. Sometimes I need to do the same thing. Place my hand right over my mouth and just let God be God. Quit doubting. Quit worrying. Quit allowing myself and my thoughts to get in the way of the great Almighty!

Who are we to contend with the One who has won it all!

Day 4

GIVE IT TO GOD

You are not what you say you are or what anyone else says you are.

You are who He says you are!

Claim that today and every day. Have you ever found yourself in a distressed situation? Jacob found himself there when he was fleeing from his brother Esau in Genesis. Then God appeared to Jacob and told him that the land which he would later name Bethel was holy ground. God told him to make an altar for Him there.

"Then let us arise and go up to Bethel, so that I may make there an altar to God who answers me in the day of my distress and has been with me wherever I have gone."
Genesis 35:3

If you are finding yourself in distress, maybe you need to put a little trust in the God who has always been with you wherever you have gone. Build yourself an altar for Him. Make a place that is yours and His. Find a quiet room, it may even be your car. Claim that as your altar for God. Give Him that space, and then begin praying. He answers us just as He did Jacob in whatever distress we may find ourselves in. He will be with us wherever we may go.

Build yourself an altar today and give it to God.

Day 5

HIGH EXPECTATIONS

Have you ever thought about the expectations we constantly put on ourselves and others? We all set expectations. Sometimes they seem like realistic ones, and sometimes, if we really thought about them, they aren't realistic at all. However, because we have set them, we get disappointed when they aren't fulfilled. We set expectations on our marriages, our kids, our friendships, and even on our jobs.

When we think our husbands should take out the trash or pick up their clothes, and they don't do it. When we feel like our kids should make certain grades, and they bring home something totally different. When we think a friend should call or text us, and they forget. At our jobs, when we feel like we should be promoted or make more money and we don't. These are everyday expectations we set, but there are other expectations we even put on ourselves.

We are constantly setting expectations, and we are constantly feeling disappointed when some of those things might not go just as we expected. Truly, are we expecting these things because of our own selfish desires or because of what we are seeking the Lord for? We should always be seeking God's will and expectations over our marriages, our children, our friendships, jobs, and life in general. It's all about our perspective.

"And now, O Lord, for what do I wait? My hope is in you."
Psalm 39:7

We need to begin to just set our expectations on God and

His will for our lives. Our God doesn't disappoint. He doesn't expect anything from us but to love and live a life honoring Him. Let your hope and expectations be set on the One who can fulfill them all.

Day 6

GRACE OF GOD

We must live by grace. Our walk with the Lord needs to be fueled by the word "grace." I really believe our lives must be structured around that word. He saved us by His grace. We are healed with grace. We are changed by His grace. He is manifested in grace, and when we are a part of Him, we become a part of the grace He offers. That grace must live inside of us.

I'm learning a lot about the word grace. I don't remember grace being showed a lot as I was growing up. We lived on pins and needles a lot hoping not to be shamed if we made a mistake, but as I grew up, my Heavenly Father has shown me so much grace. The more I realize the importance of that word, the more I realize that I also must always be willing to pour out grace onto others. Whether it's praying for God's grace upon them or offering the grace of God just as God offers us.

God is made of grace. When he sent His Son to die for us, He sent us grace. Grace is the unmerited favor of God. Do you realize that you live with that favor every day, no matter what?

yet not I, but the grace of God that was with me.
1 Corinthians 15:10 (NIV)

We have God's grace within us. When things seem to be ungraceful within our lives, God's grace is there to put the pieces back together. Allow yourself to truly feel the grace that God offers you today.

Journal

Day 7

Take time to meditate on God's word. What's on your heart this week?

_____

_____

_____

_____

_____

_____

_____

_____

_____

_____

_____

_____

_____

_____

_____

_____

_____

_____

Week Thirty-Four

Day 1

POWER OF INFLUENCE

Have you ever thought about yourself and how you are an influencer?

Are you influencing others toward God or away from Him?

Are others being influenced more toward Jesus through what we are pouring out or more driven in the flesh for what we're not pouring in?

We all have the opportunity every day to influence those around us, no matter our age. We can drive others closer to God or further away. Do we set an example of characteristics of the Lord for others by not gossiping, showing love even when we don't feel like it, forgiving, accepting, or nourishing those into His word?

We think about how much our kids can be influenced by peer pressure, but even as adults we can be easily influenced, if we aren't careful, by those we surround ourselves with. Then that same influence can be what we start to instill in our kids without us even realizing it.

How are you influencing others? Think about it.

Let's influence others to be drawn closer to the Lord!

"In the same way, let your light shine before others, so that they may see your good works and give glory to your Father who is in heaven."
Matthew 5:16

Day 2

ALWAYS A PROCESS

At times it can seem like we are all alone. We know God is with us, but we can't feel His presence. Sometimes we must find Him in our situation.

Are we truly seeking Him exactly where we are in our situation, or are we just asking Him to fix it because we don't want to live in it?

If any of you lacks wisdom, let him ask God, who gives generously to all without approach, and it will be given to him. But let him ask in faith, with no doubting, for the one who doubts is like a wave of the sea that is driven and tossed in the wind. James 1:5-6

Being tossed, pulled, and prodded by our problems can cause us to forget that there is always a process. God does everything for a reason. When you struggle to see God in your situations, you are struggling to know how faithful He really is. You may be forgetting just what His faithfulness has already done for you. God makes no mistakes.

To find God in your circumstance, you must be willing to open your mind to believing exactly who He is. He's the God of our todays and tomorrows. He's a God with no ending. He's a God made of love, grace, and mercy. He is a God that will protect and calm. Our God is our Creator, and He has all the capability to show Himself to us, but we must be willing to accept that and find Him.

Seek, pray, and allow His works to be shown to you.

Day 3

PREPARE FOR BATTLE

If you were going into one of our armed forces before being sent to war, you would be trained and conditioned. When joining a branch of service, you would first attend basic training and then a more intensive training, depending on your job. No one would want to be sent out to war without proper training. I can only say for myself, but I don't know how prepared I would feel even with the most intensive training and conditioning.

In life we go through different kinds of wars within ourselves or our life's circumstances. These wars can be mental or physical. Some of these wars last a lifetime, and some can be quick battles. The Lord begins to train and condition us from before birth.

"Before I formed you in the womb I knew you, before you were born I set you apart; I appointed you as a prophet to the nations."
Jeremiah 1:5(NIV)

I think we sometimes forget the work He has done and continues to do inside of us until after the battle is over, after we see the victory. Truthfully, there are times when we can't see the victory, but God has already claimed it over our lives.

Blessed be the Lord, my rock, who trains my hands for war, and my fingers for battle. Psalm 144:1

I can personally say there have been many times in my own life when I have felt so unprepared for the battle at hand. I have quickly forgotten who I have been in training with.

Who has conditioned me and prepared me for the battle? I think if we truly remembered that every time, we wouldn't be scared when the wars arise.

He has trained our hands for war and our fingers for battle.

I don't know if you are fighting a battle today, but I want you to remind yourself of the One who has equipped and trained your body and mind for whatever you may be facing or may face in the future.

You have been trained and conditioned by The Most High. You are more ready then you could ever be to CLAIM THIS VICTORY!

Day 4

FUEL YOUR MOTIVATION

Do you lack motivation? There are many times I lack the motivation to want to do house chores or to just get up and go to work, for that matter.

Can you think of things you do when you lack motivation?

I will put stuff off. I hit the snooze button. Sometimes I can even pull out of my excuse box a reason why it would be a better idea to just do it later. I think I thought of every excuse there was not to just finish this devotional. We feed ourselves with things to keep us unmotivated. When we feel motivated to do something, it's usually not a task to get it done.

What are you allowing to drain your motivation?

And whatever you do, in word or deed, do everything in the name of the Lord Jesus, giving thanks to God the Father through him.
Colossians 3:17

We lack nothing with God. Even when we feel like we are unmotivated, if we start to feed ourselves with the word or with worship, God will motivate our hearts to do even the simplest task. I want you to try it. The next time you are unmotivated to get up out of bed, turn some upbeat worship music on, and see if it lifts your spirits. Take a few minutes before doing something, and just give thanks to God for being able to do it. Whatever you do in word or deed, do it in the name Jesus! Find your motivation within Him.

Day 5

COME OUT

When Jesus raises Lazarus from the dead in John 11:36-44, Martha is in unbelief of what she is about to see. She knows he has been dead for four days, and she doesn't believe that he could possibly be alive behind the stone. Jesus speaks to Martha and says,

"Did I not tell you that if you believe, you will see the glory of God?"
John 11:40

I think our belief of what God is capable of becomes weak because our sight on what He has already done has become distant. Have you forgotten how He has already moved in your life?

Martha here is just like us. She is doubting what God is truly capable of. We do the same thing in life. We forget about the ways he has already moved and start to doubt what He still can do. Jesus tells her, though, that it takes nothing but belief to see the glory of God.

When he had said this, Jesus called in a loud voice, "Lazarus, come out!" John 11:43

That "come out" should mean something to us. We need to come out of our unbelief. God is capable of everything. What do you need to have a little belief in today to see the true glory of God? Come out of your unbelief! God is wanting to raise your unbelief to life!

Day 6

AMEN

Today let's share a prayer together.

"For where two or three are gathered in my name, there am I among them." Matthew 18:20

Dear Heavenly Father,

Thank You. Thank You for Your love that You continuously pour out onto us. Lord, today I want to come to You in thanks and in praise. In thanks for all You have done and continue to do. In praise for what You have shown me, how You have loved me, and where You have brought me. Lord, I also want to come to You for each individual person reading this book. I want to come to You for their needs, their worries, their trials, and their frustrations. I want to come to You over their fears, their struggles, their loss of hope, and their hearts. Lord, I ask You that whatever each one of them may be going through, whether it is positive or negative, that they learn to embrace You in their now. Lord, I pray that they begin to feel Your presence and peace. Lord, I pray for a movement to happen in areas that they have been waiting for. I pray for healing to begin to transform their minds and bodies. I pray that they begin to throw themselves into You in the midst of all of their struggles. I pray that they begin to let go of anything holding them back in their relationship with You. Lord, I know You are all-powerful. You are capable of breaking chains that they have held onto for years. You are capable of healing, restoring, and providing a way where there seems to be no way. Lord, You are a good, good Father, and I believe You are working miracles through this

prayer. You are making ways where some have not seen ways in a long time. You are working on hearts. You are mending relationships. You are healing bodies and transforming lives. Lord, You are a miracle worker! Lord, I come to You today knowing that what You are doing through each of their lives is bigger than comprehension. You are allowing them to love, be loved, and forgive with the same forgiveness You have shown us through Your grace every day! You are doing things they may not be able to see, but Lord, the transformations will be heart felt. Thank You, Lord. We praise You, Lord! I love You and give You all the praise, glory, and honor!

AMEN

Journal

Day 7

Take time to meditate on God's word. What's on your heart this week?

_____

_____

_____

_____

_____

_____

_____

_____

_____

_____

_____

_____

_____

_____

_____

_____

_____

_____

_____

_____

Week Thirty-Five

Day 1

WE MATTER TO HIM

How often do we feel forgotten about? I know there have been times in my life when I have wondered, "Do I even matter?" We all go through periods where we think, "Does anyone even care?" That's where our faith plays a part in our walk. I believe God wants us to hear from Him before we hear from others. To me that means believing in what He says we are over what people may say.

As our pastor once said, "God is bragging on us telling us we are doing better than we think we are." - Pastor Brandon Teachey

You do matter. Even when you just go to work, you matter. Even when you are taking care of your kids or your spouse, and it seems that no one sees what you do, you do matter. Everything that you do matters because God sees it all. How you do it matters. How you see yourself matters to God. God wants us to see ourselves in Him.

God wants you to know you matter today. Even if you don't think anyone sees what you are doing, God does! He sees your efforts, your hard work, and your determination. He sees what you do behind closed doors, and He sees what you do for His kingdom. God sees it all, and He says you matter. You matter to me, too!

In him we were also chosen, having been predestined according to the plan of him who works out everything in conformity with the purpose of his will, in order that we, who were the first to put our hope in Christ, might be for the praise of his glory. Ephesians 1:11-12 (NIV)

Day 2

YOU HAVE ENOUGH

Maybe you have heard of the story of Jesus feeding the 5,000. In John 6 Jesus performs a miracle for 5,000 people by feeding them off five loaves and two fish.

Jesus then took the loaves, and when he had given thanks, he distributed them to those who were seated. So also the fish, as much as they wanted. John 6:11

Sometimes what we have may seem too little in our eyes. Even the disciples were confused by how Jesus was going to feed all those people with just that amount of food, but just like in our own lives when we think we don't have enough of what it takes, that's when the supernatural steps in.

Jesus gave thanks first. Sometimes that's what we need to stop and do. Give thanks for what we do have. Whether it seems too little or not. We often get caught up in the "I don't have enough" mindset. "I don't have enough strength to get through this." "I don't have what it takes to do that." "The money or the resources aren't there." If God has given it to you to do, you have more than enough to do it.

And when they have eaten their fill, He told His disciples, "Gather up the leftover fragments, that nothing may be lost." So they gathered them up and filled twelve baskets with fragments from five barley loaves left by those who had eaten. John 6:12-13

I can think of past times where I have thought, "I don't have what I need to get through this," but on the other side of that same situation I realized that I had leftover fragments. I had enough because my God is enough!

Day 3

WHAT WE'VE BECOME

Could you imagine if we wore our sin on the outside of us? The things we've done or the mistakes we've made? Some people still do. They look in the mirror every day, and they may not physically see the sin, but they see it in their heads when they see themselves. They see what they've done or who they used to be, but that's not who the Father says they are and what they can be.

I am glad that we don't have to look in the mirror and see what we were, but we can look in the mirror with confidence in Christ and see what we've become. We can see we have been cleansed and set free. We have been washed as white as snow. We no longer reflect our sin, but we reflect a forgiving God.

Are you reflecting Him? What do you see when you look in the mirror?

"Come now, let us reason together, says the Lord: though your sins are like scarlet, they shall be as white as snow; though they are red like crimson, they shall become like wool." Isaiah 1:18

Day 4

WRITE YOUR VOWS

At a wedding there are always some form of vows performed. It doesn't matter how big or small the wedding, the couple performs vows in front of either guests or just for each other. This is their declaration of love and what they are promising to do between the two of them and God.

In my own wedding, we wrote our own vows and declared them over our marriage with our friends and family there, but, most importantly, knowing that God was also standing with us.

Have you ever thought about writing vows to God?

This actually crossed my mind; how we could declare our love for Him and what we want to vow as a promise to Him.

This is something I want to work on to love and honor Him for all He has given me.

So will I ever sing praises to your name, as I perform my vows day after day. Psalm 61:8

I challenge you to sit down and write a vow out to God sometime. A shout of praise and a vow for all you want to do for Him in your days here. For better or for worse. As we all know, life will throw us our worst at times. Then perform them daily for Him in prayer and in praise; declaring your love for Him day after day.

Day 5

AWAKEN YOUR SOUL

As I was sitting with God one morning, and my husband's alarm was sounding in the background as it does every day, I felt that there was something different about this morning. Have you ever felt that way? You have woken up and thought, "You know what? There is something different about today?!"

It crossed my mind that today is the day. Today is the day to wake up, not in just an "I'm getting out of bed, going through the same routine of getting ready, and getting out the door" type of way. Today is the day I'm going to wake up. I'm going to have an awakening inside of me, and I'm going to listen to the beat of God's given noise all around me. I'm going to take in the noises, the smells, and the scenery. I'm going to awaken the inside to allow God's presence of who He is, what He's done, and the creations He has made to start to engulf and indwell inside of me. I want today to be different. Isn't that the choice He has given us every day? I want today to not be beating against the same drum as every other day. I want today's motions to be done in better purpose. I want today to be driven in my senses. I want to wake up those things we don't choose to wake up every day because we don't think of it. I want to walk in my full purpose today.

Today, I'm choosing to not just give parts of me but ALL of me, truly taking in the presence of God in His fullness. Will you choose to do this with me?

You are observing special days and months and seasons and years!
Galatians 4:10 (NIV)

Day 6

HIT THE PAUSE BUTTON

The Holy Spirit put into my heart one day that I needed to hit the pause button. Not the snooze where you delay doing something, but the pause where you take in that one screenshot. In life God gives us a lot of important one-time screenshots that we can quickly forget about or not fully take in because we are so wrapped up in just getting through our days. Life is hectic, and instead of pausing in the goodness, we get wrapped up with the play button.

Life is continuously on play, but we don't need to forget to pause sometimes. In the pause is when mindful thinking can begin to take place. Captured thoughts begin to process through us, and the details of what God is doing can start to be inscribed in us.

Isn't it funny how we think that because our lives are so busy, we don't get the choice of pausing? God gives us the choice every day to see Him in his entirety; we can either choose to say yes or to just not slow down.

I used to talk about how I wished I could pause my kids growing up; I could just keep them at a certain age. However, I can choose to pause where I am with them and take in the moment deeper; realizing everything else can wait! That's exactly what God wants us to do. Enjoy those moments He gives us, realizing when our time is with Him, everything else can wait.

When He is pouring into us with people, at church, and in our alone time, everything else can truly take the backseat and we can hit the pause button. Take in those moments

He gives you to pour out and the moments He is pouring into you. Let's try to learn to hit the pause button and truly take in the goodness He gives us every day!

But I have calmed and quieted my soul, like a weaned child with its mother; like a weaned child is my soul within me.
Psalm 131:2

Journal

Day 7

Take time to meditate on God's word. What's on your heart this week?

_____

_____

_____

_____

_____

_____

_____

_____

_____

_____

_____

_____

_____

_____

_____

_____

_____

_____

_____

Week Thirty-Six

Day 1

CHANGE YOUR IF

When we are held under the fire, we think, "Why me, or when is this going to end?" This is when God is taking us and creating in us something with more clarity, something that shines just a little brighter. We are able to see Him just a little more. This is when we realize that we need Him more, and our ashes are what make our testimony that much more powerful.

Think about Eve. When you bring her name up, sometimes you may hear others say, "If she wouldn't have eaten that fruit, the world would be different." That "if" statement actually doesn't just get thrown around with Eve. It gets thrown around with us now. We say it in our own lives, "If I wouldn't have done that, then…"

We say it with our kids, "If they just would have listened, then…"

There's also the, "If I could have then maybe..."

The "ifs" we use always go with a "then" after them. For instance, in my own life I used to say, "If my parents wouldn't have gotten divorced, THEN maybe I wouldn't have grown up in an abusive household." Those ifs can get dirty and downright mind-numbing if you ask me.

Don't get caught up on the ifs!

They can become a heavy load to carry. They can play on your own insecurities, or sometimes even put you in a state of depression. You think about it. If you are always saying,

"If this, then this wouldn't have occurred," you aren't stopping to think about the positive the if can bring.

Yes, Eve ate the fruit, but Jesus took the weight of our sin on the cross.

Yes, my parents were divorced, but I am living and walking proof that God is real.

A lot of our ifs can be turned around by just a small perspective switch.

The enemy tries to make us forget that.

And we know that in all things God works for the good of those who love him, who have been called according to his purpose.
Romans 8:28 (NIV)

Day 2

RULE OVER IT

In the story of Cain and Abel, Adam and Eve's sons, it seems that one brother is in competition with the other. They both brought the Lord offerings, and the Lord took Abel's, causing Cain to get angry.

The Lord said to Cain, "Why are you angry, and why has your face fallen? If you do well, will you not be accepted? And if you do not do well, sin is crouching at the door. It's desire is contrary to you, but you must rule over it."
Genesis 4:6-7

If something was crouching at the front door of your house, you wouldn't be able to see it as well as you would if it was standing tall, and you could look out the window or a peep hole at it. That's what sin does to us. The enemy has it crouching so that it's not so visible, but it's still right there. If you were to open the door, what is crouching outside of it is still going to be right there ready to come in.

Cain ended up allowing the sin in.

Is there sin crouching at your door today? In our own lives, we allow sin to crouch at the door to our hearts. We have possibly even allowed it to rule over us at times, but that's not God's desire for us. The enemy's or the world's desire is for the sin to rule you, but God's desire is for you to rule over it! What are you allowing to rule over you? Sin comes in many forms. For Cain it came in jealousy. Today, take back control over God's desire for you.

Day 3

POWER & AUTHORITY

The voice of the Lord is powerful. His voice made things happen, and today His voice claims over us a new day. I am in awe that even as the sun rose this morning, God said, "Let it rise." Even as we got out of bed today, despite what yesterday may have held or what we even may face today, God said, "Let them rise."

His voice speaks with power and authority. Not just over the mountains He moves, but through the air that He circulates inside of us to move. He begins a work inside of us every day. One that can reflect who He is. He gives us free will over that reflection.

I don't know about you, but I want to be in awe of Him every day. The newness He has spoken into today, the praises that the birds are singing, the softness of His voice, are all awe inspiring. That through His gentleness we were created, and through that same gentleness He is restoring us piece by piece.

I am in awe of what overflows from Him into us every day. What is good and true. That's the gentleness of His love for you and me.

Let's be in awe.

Let all the earth fear the Lord; let all the inhabitants stand in awe of him! Psalm 33:8

Day 4

HE CLEARS THE CLUTTER

I just love when God sends those little winks or reminders, and when we are in tune to hearing them so clearly. If you are anything like me, sometimes our heads are filled with way too much clutter that things don't seem so easy to perceive.

He spoke with me so plainly one day and reminded me of His goodness when I heard two others speak about how clearly, they had heard His voice as well. Isn't it funny how we can get so caught up in all the color that God is just black and white? A lot of times, we complicate things in our brains and make things more difficult than they have to be.

We like to shade and color things in with our thoughts, and we distort the picture of what God wants us to see. His faithfulness shines through so brightly by just the small whisper of His voice.

It's amazing that no matter how much clutter may be taking over in our lives, when God speaks, He clears the clutter!

"Call to me and I will answer you, and will tell you great and hidden things that you have not known." Jeremiah 33:3

Day 5

A PIECE OF JESUS

We have probably all heard the saying, "Sharing is caring." We tell it to our kids when they are young, and I'm sure our parents have said it to us once or twice. In our walk with Jesus, that is spot on as the truth.

I'm a sharer of all things most of the time.

There is one thing I don't like to share all the time, and that's food when I'm really hangry (you know, hungry and angry put together).

The Lord wants us to share His word and His truth all the time without hesitation, not saying no to anyone. Truly if that saying could be used anywhere it's in our walk with the Lord.

Sharing our hearts to others around us is caring for those around us. What we know about the Lord could make a huge impact on someone else's life. Sharing is caring when it comes to the Lord.

Let's give those around us a piece of Jesus.

But be doers of the word, and not hearers only, deceiving yourselves.
James 1:22

Day 6

MADE FOR PARADISE

Can you imagine yourself in a perfect world - a world before sin came in, a world with no heartache or shame, or a world not filled with tears or pain? Have you ever tried to picture that?

That's the world that God has for us in heaven. A place that is full of peace. A place where love just encompasses us.

We were made for paradise.

What happiness we experience here is nothing compared to the joy our hearts will experience one day in paradise. Those places we visit here that we think are paradise are nothing compared to where God has created us to spend eternity.

This such a beautiful promise - no matter where you are now, this is not your forever home.

"My home is in heaven, I'm just passing through this world."- Billy Graham

Our paradise awaits us!

For here we have no lasting city, but we seek the city that is to come.
Hebrews 13:14

Journal

Day 7

Take time to meditate on God's word. What's on your heart this week?

_____

_____

_____

_____

_____

_____

_____

_____

_____

_____

_____

_____

_____

_____

_____

_____

_____

_____

_____

_____

Week Thirty-Seven

Day 1

INSERT YOUR NAME

"Fear not, for I have redeemed you; I have called you by name, you are mine." Isaiah 43:1

When I read that scripture, I couldn't help but think that the same authority and possession He claims here over Israel, He has also claimed over us.

He tells us to fear not; He has already saved us from the sin of this world through His blood on the cross at Calvary.

He has called us by name.

Have you ever thought about the significance of your name? In the Bible people were actually named based on their significance. Sometimes they may have even been renamed.

Do you realize your name has meaning to God? He calls you directly by name, which means He has established importance in it. He speaks life when He speaks, and that means when He calls you, He calls you His.

It makes me think of those times we call our children because they are in trouble. We don't usually just say their first name, we say their first, middle, and last. I think God calls us with the same emphasis.

"I have called you by name, you are mine." Insert your name in that today!

Day 2

HEAT OF LIFE'S FURNANCE

Have you ever sat in front of a fire? Sometimes one side gets a little hotter than the other, and you may get up to move. Sometimes you may even back away from the fire all together. Life can be a lot like a fire at times. The heat of life's furnace gets turned up and you're like, "Lord I feel like backing away, hiding away, or even disappearing. I like the more comfortable temperatures. Let's keep it on 75 degrees."

In this you rejoice, though now for a little while, if necessary, you have been grieved by various trials, so that the tested genuineness of your faith-more precious than gold that perishes though it is tested by fire-may be found to result in praise and glory and honor at the revelation of Jesus Christ. 1 Peter 1:6-7

I pray that I'm always open to the refining that God wants to do in and through me. Even if that means my furnace may become too hot at times.

We feel like our impurities lessen our value, or our trials may seem forgotten, but just as pennies make a dollar, we truly make up a lot to God. We are His children. We may not see the value of ourselves or our current situations, but the genuineness of our faith is more precious than gold.

Gold is tried through a furnace and can come out without losing anything, but it also comes out with nothing gained. Our faith is tried through a furnace and can come out even more glorious and richer than before. The heat may be "turnt up" in your life, and you may find yourself in a fiery

furnace, but that just means God is purifying you! Just as the scripture says, "In this you REJOICE!"

And just as pennies make a dollar, we too make a difference no matter where we've been or where we are today!!

Day 3

EXPERIENCING JESUS CHRIST

God has created a way for us to experience Him every day. The experience changes through the discipline we create in our lives for Him to come in. All throughout the Bible, people experience Jesus Christ. They encounter Him. The circumstance for the encounter with Him is always different depending on how much we are willing to open ourselves up on the receiving end. What always remains the same is what He shows us constantly, and that is love.

We all find ourselves in different places right now in our lives. The world will continue to revolve even when our hearts seem to stop. The world continues to try to satisfy something only our creator was meant to.

We should create a space for Him through our discipline so that we can encounter His everlasting presence every day.

We create habits that make limited space for our full potential with the Lord. We have to create a clean environment for Him. Limiting the space for outside things in our hearts.

This takes discipline!

This is our prayer today,

Create in me a clean heart, O God, and renew a right spirit within
me. Psalm 51:10

Day 4

PERFECTED IN FAITH

Maybe you have heard this next scripture.

"But take heart; I have overcome the world."
John 16:33

I think our form of overcoming is perfected in our faith.

For everyone who has been born of God overcomes the world. And this is the victory that has overcome the world-our faith. 1 John 5:4

Did you read that like I did? Everyone who has been born of God overcomes the world. We have overcome those spirits of fear and those spirits of defeat. Who knows, you may even fight spirits of anger or of judgement. You have already been deemed an overcomer. The scripture didn't just say some, it says everyone who has been born of God overcomes the world.

Do you believe that?

Do you believe that the victory over all those ugly things our minds fight lies within our faith?

All we have to do is claim that victory.

Day 5

DELAYED EMOTIONS

Life hits us like a ton of bricks at times. Instead of feeling like sunshine, it feels like it knocks the breath out of us.

You feel crippled by your situation.

Have you been there? You can't seem to catch your breath where you are.

For a lot of us, it seems that our emotions can pile up really fast. Or maybe you are like me, sometimes I have a thing called "delayed emotions." I'm usually trying to stand tall and strong for those around me, but when the seas calm and I get by myself, I begin to process everything.

However, we may fight the inevitable of life, we may feel crippled where we are.

Didn't Jesus heal a crippled man? (Matthew 9)

When we feel beaten down or drained in our situation, God will come to us right where we are. He will heal all those crippled parts of us.

God is always purifying what is His.

"I will put my trust in him." Hebrews 2:13

Day 6

WORK YOUR SCHEDULE

Last night I started thinking about all the time we have in a day, but we still use that saying, "There's not enough time in a day."

We have 1 day
24 hours
1440 minutes
86400 seconds

As I broke down sleep time (8 hours), work or volunteer time (another 8 hours), Then drive time to and from, kids' activities, house chores, or other misc. times you can think of, I subtracted another 5 hours from that. Leaving us with a total of 3 hours of time unaccounted for. You may say I have no unaccounted-for time, but I say I challenge you to sit down and work your schedule. Our days, hours, minutes, and seconds are super crucial in our walk with the Lord. As I lay in bed one night, I couldn't help but think how much time I waste away. Yes, I took time to relax and catch a breath from my last couple weeks of straight busyness, but the seconds, minutes, and even hours, not just yesterday, but every day that I "wasted away."

It is crucial in our walk to always be evaluating what we are giving to the Lord. What we are sacrificing for Him, and how we can serve Him. One of those areas of sacrifice is time. How much time do you give Him?

So teach us to number our days that we may get a heart of wisdom.
Psalm 90:12

I don't know about you, but I want a heart full of wisdom, and in order to have that, I know I must number my days by hours, minutes, and seconds. In school, straight-A's didn't come without work. A straight-A heart for God isn't going to come without dedication. In order to get a heart of wisdom, we have to put in the time.

Join me in reevaluating our time.

Journal

Day 7

Take time to meditate on God's word. What's on your heart this week?

_____

_____

_____

_____

_____

_____

_____

_____

_____

_____

_____

_____

_____

_____

_____

_____

_____

_____

_____

Week Thirty-Eight

Day 1

MAKE ROOM

Last week we talked about wasted time. Today I want to hit on wasted space.

I love to take pictures, but every now and then I may be at an event or on vacation and my camera or phone memory card says it's full. I then have to spend time figuring out which pictures I can delete and which ones I want to keep. It can be fun looking back at the memories, but it can also be sad or upsetting, depending on what kind of memories you are revisiting.

How full is your memory card this morning? Better yet, what's your memory card full of?

Set your minds on things above, not on things that are on earth.
Colossians 3:2

What do we have in our minds that is taking up space that God has intended for Him? It's important for us to clean up, clear out, and delete some things every now and then. Just as it's important that we be careful of what we allow in, in the first place.

God has intended for us to have a sound mind. Is there something today that's not allowing you to have what He has intended? Visit it, pray about it, and ask God to delete anything that's not of Him or holds you back from your full potential with Him. It's time to clear some things out of your memory card that are not of God.

Day 2

THE BEST WIN

Therefore the Lord waits to be gracious to you, and therefore he exalts himself to show mercy to you.
Isaiah 30:18

"Waits to be gracious?" What if I need Him now? I don't have time to wait for graciousness.

We've all been there. A place where we think we don't have time to wait for the Lord's answers or the Lord's direction because, in our minds, we need an answer right this minute. How are we supposed to say, "yes or no" to that person when we don't even know what we want to answer? We've prayed about it, but the confirmation or direction we are looking for still hasn't come from God.

The older I get, the more I realize that waiting isn't always a bad thing. As much as I would like answers right away sometimes it's in the waiting that we learn even more than just the answer we were searching for in the beginning.

This verse also says, "He exalts Himself to show mercy to you."

He raises Himself to show compassion, grace, and forgiveness toward us so that the graciousness of the answer in the wait may be revealed. Waiting for God's graciousness causes you to let go of the "RIGHT NOW" and rely on the "BEST WHEN." When you let His graciousness be your answer it truly is the "BEST WIN" for your life.

Day 3

CALL OUT IN PRAYER

My heart is heavy for prayer. Today, I challenge you guys to get to a quiet space and spend some time in prayer. If you don't know what to pray, ask God to help you in your prayer life. If you have a hard time praying, get to a quiet space, and just ask God to come to where you are. Sometimes just sitting in that quiet space and closing your eyes without saying a word can fill you with a peaceful and overwhelming calmness from the presence of God like no other. Don't use any excuses. I know it's hard sometimes to get a minute of quiet time, but today find just a few minutes for yourself and God. Don't allow the enemy to steal the time you have with God. He loves to tell you lies and make you think, but God has something so great to tell you today, even if it's just to remind you of how much He loves you.

Go to Him in prayer today.

I call on you, my God, for you will answer me; turn your ear to me and hear my prayer. Psalm 17:6 (NIV)

Day 4

BALANCING ACT

Have you ever tried to balance something? Makes me think of those relay games where you take an egg and balance it on a spoon, trying to walk fast to get to the next person without dropping and cracking the egg. Doesn't life feel like a relay at times? Better yet, a balancing act? You have so many things going on that you are just trying to get through to the next thing so someone else can maybe take over.

God didn't intend for us to go through life feeling like we are in a relay or a balancing act. God intends for His control to be our balance.

Balance in life is a good thing, but true balance doesn't come from an act, it comes from knowing who has the egg. Sometimes what we are needing is less control of our own balance, while putting trust in the One who is in control.

What are some things you are trying to balance? Are you in a balancing act or relay race? If so, try shifting the weight of the balance onto Him. Getting our balance under control sometimes just means making a shift.

A false balance is an abomination to the Lord, but a just weight is his delight. Proverbs 11:1

Day 5

A DAY IN OUR SHOES

I don't know about you, but I love the fact that Jesus, the Savior of the world, put Himself in our shoes to feel what we feel daily. If you have never read the story of Jesus being tempted in the wilderness, it's a good one, and you should spend just a couple minutes today reading it.

After Jesus was baptized by John in the Book of Matthew, He went into the wilderness, and after He had fasted for forty days and forty nights, He was tempted by the devil.

Don't you feel the same sometimes? You feel like you are doing all the right things, but the enemy seems to come in even stronger with temptations. What's interesting to me is that Satan didn't try to attack until he thought Jesus was weak.

Every time the enemy came at Him, Jesus replied with what was already written in the word. (Deut. 8:3, Deut. 6:16)

What does this teach us? Every time the enemy tries to come at us, we have to know what's in the word. When the enemy comes in with temptations in our own wilderness, we have to be ready to basically say, "You are a liar; this is what my God says and is written in His holy word."

The enemy can't fight the truth. He is just trying to see if you know it. As the enemy tried to tempt Him a third time, this is what Jesus says.

Then Jesus said to him, "Be gone, Satan!" Matthew 4:10

What do you need to tell the enemy to "be gone" from in your life today? Say it. Speak it. Give life to the words that come out of your mouth and tell him to be gone. Then follow it by scripture and tell him why he has to.

Day 6

OUR FIRST

Sometimes things just don't go as planned - some mornings are like that for me. I wake up with all intentions of doing certain things, and then time seems to speed up, and I can't get any of it done. It is as if I am facing opposition after opposition. My computer goes "kerplunk." If I told you how many times, I tried to send a devotion one morning to my email list on the iPad, you probably wouldn't believe me. As things kept coming, it was as if God whispered, "I'm first."

I was quickly reminded of this scripture.

In their hearts humans plan their course, but the Lord establishes their steps. Proverbs 16:9 (NIV)

He is our first step. My plan for this particular morning wasn't going as expected, but God's was. He wanted to establish my first steps.

Sometimes we just need to pray in those instances. Lord, I have planned things out, and those things aren't going as planned; but, Lord, Your plan establishes the right steps for my life. I ask You, Lord, to direct each and every one of my steps that puts You first. His plans far outweigh our own. So, if you get bogged down today or even this week in frustration from your plans not quite working out "as planned," stop and pray. Remember our God is not a God of frustration and that His steps should always be our first.

Journal

Day 7

Take time to meditate on God's word. What's on your heart this week?

_____

_____

_____

_____

_____

_____

_____

_____

_____

_____

_____

_____

_____

_____

_____

_____

_____

_____

_____

_____

_____

Week Thirty-Nine

Day 1

STAY AWAKE

I'm a routine type of girl. I like schedules. As I spoke with one of my friends one day, I was reminded through our conversation about how we need to "stay awake."

God puts things in front of us every day that our eyes and hearts are meant to observe, but our minds get so busy that we don't even notice. It's so important that we stay awake for those reminders, those gifts, that He gives us as a sweet embrace of His love. These are things we can share to encourage others.

Are you truly awake today? Have you awakened what God has put inside of you for you to see - His sweet reminders for you in this day or His sweet whispers of goodness? Are you sweeping by not feeling, seeing, or discerning what God has for you?

"Awake, O sleeper, and arise from the dead, and Christ will shine on you." Look carefully then how you walk, not as unwise but as wise, making best use of the time, because the days are evil.
Ephesians 5:14-16

I also love the Message translation of this verse.

Wake up from your sleep, climb out your coffins; Christ will show you light! So watch your step. Use your head. Make most of every chance you get. These are desperate times!
Ephesians 5:14-16 (MSG)

It tells us what to do. Wake up and step out of your

sin. Christ is going to show you His light. Watch where you go and use your head. This is my favorite part - "make most of every chance you get." These are hard times because all the things around us can consume us, but when we stay awake in God, He has some pretty amazing things for us. Awaken what He has put in you today.

Day 2

DEEPEST SORROW

When Jesus was sorrowful and troubled before His crucifixion, He went alone to pray.

> *"My soul is sorrowful even to death, even to death."*
> *Matthew 26:38*

Sorrow is something we all face here on Earth. It's something Jesus faced for us, even to death. Jesus felt the sorrow of what was about to happen. Even still, what did He do? He went to pray alone.

When Jesus prayed, it wasn't with selfish ambition.

> *And going a little farther he fell on his face and prayed, saying, "My Father, if it be possible, let this cup pass from me; nevertheless, not as I will, but as you will."*
> *Matthew 26:39*

"Nevertheless, if this is something You don't take away, Lord, I want Your will for my life and not my own." This should be our own prayer.

He knew that it wasn't His will, but it was the will of God, His Father. Even with the sorrow he felt while facing death for you and me, He prayed, "God, Your will, not My own." When Jesus went away to pray and then came back, His disciples, who He had asked to pray with Him, were sleeping.

Jesus told Peter,

"Watch and pray that you may not enter into temptation. The spirit indeed is willing, but the flesh is weak."
Matthew 26:41

When we are facing deep sorrow, our spirit knows our need, but our flesh is weak. How many times do we deny prayer when God is calling us to seek Him? Jesus knew in this time of sorrow the only thing He could do was pray.

Day 3

WHERE YOUR FEET GO

Have you heard the quote, "Before you criticize someone, walk a mile in their shoes? That way you'll be a mile from them, and you'll have their shoes."?

One night during youth group, we read in Joshua 1, and the scripture talks about how after Moses' death, the Lord tells Joshua to go lead his people through many places.

"Every place that the sole of your foot will tread upon I have given to you, just as I promised to Moses."
Joshua 1:3

Have you ever thought about that in the context of your own walk? Everywhere the soles of our feet go, God has given to us. I sometimes forget that. No matter where I am and no matter where I have been, God has given me every road that I have traveled.

"Do not turn from it to the right hand or to the left, that you may have good success wherever you go."
Joshua 1:7

I have turned different ways, but still God has always placed me right back on track. This is a good reminder to us that not mediocre success, but good success will be with us when we travel with God and stay His path for our lives.

God travels with us everywhere the soles of our feet go. He doesn't just walk a mile in our shoes, he walks everywhere with us in our shoes. God knows more than anyone; he knows us deeper than ourselves. Remember as you are

walking through your day, that every place the sole of your feet will tread upon has been given to you by your Heavenly Father.

Day 4

CARRIES US THROUGH

It's a beautiful thing to me to see how we all come together in times of tragedy. Even before hurricanes may come in our state, we have all kinds of people coming in from different states to help wherever we may need them. I think that everyone tends to see the bad in these situations a lot more than they do the good. It's easy to do knowing the potential of the storm.

This gives me a lot of insight into why God doesn't always give us all the fine details of our own lives' storms. Could you imagine if you had someone telling you everything that was going to happen leading up to and after a particular sickness, or if you had someone telling you what was going to happen as your children got older through the course of their actions? I mean, we would all be basket cases running around trying to figure out what we were going to do to prep for these things.

I am thankful He doesn't do that. As much as I would like to know, I'm thankful that He carries me through the process knowing that each step has to be taken with Him.

God is in all the details, even the super fine ones.

The steps of a man are established by the Lord, when he delights in his way. Psalm 37:23

Day 5

WRAPPED UP IN NORMALITY

One night I lay in bed long after everyone else was asleep and couldn't seem to get myself to shut down. It wasn't because we didn't have power. It wasn't because I was hungry or thirsty, and it wasn't because I just wanted a warm shower or a hot meal. I didn't feel scared or worried. It was strictly because I felt guilty. Guilty that I didn't feel all those things anymore. I was fed. We did have power again. We weren't in need of anything. My family was all together; we were safe and sound in the presence of each other, but there were others who weren't.

Don't get me wrong, my heart was grateful, and I thanked God for blessing us, but my heart also felt some guilt.

Guilt for taking so much for granted when others are dealing with some of these struggles on a daily basis. Guilt that I wasn't helping more. It was just overwhelming. I started to pray and talk to God through it. A part of me didn't know if it was the enemy trying to beat me down or God trying to open my eyes.

I know I can get caught up in the normality of every day. I believe that I get so caught up in it that sometimes I may even forget to be more intentional in acknowledging my blessings. How many times have I thanked God, but truly not given the thanks He deserves? I realized that maybe sometimes I don't really grasp just how blessed I am because it is so easy to get wrapped up in the normality of what I do have.

I began to try to figure out how I could help more. How

could I show God more gratitude?

How easy would it be to offer kind words or water to those in need? How easy would it be to feed people who are working hard or offer time to volunteer?

I love seeing how tragedy pulls us together, but then again, is that what it should take for us to step out of our normality and into the need of right now?

It's the simplest thing, but such a blessing, to have a pen and paper on which to write down my heart. I want to be deliberate in giving thanks for even the "little" things - feeling the air blowing against my feet below me and being able to hear the sounds of the birds outside singing their praises.

I want to be less normal. I want to stop getting wrapped up in my normality that I forget this may not be normal for others.

I want to be used even on a normal day because my normal day may be someone else's tragedy.

You will be enriched in every way to be generous in every way, which
through us will produce thanksgiving to God.
2 Corinthians 9:11

Day 6

WHEN TO SAY NO

Everything is not for us. Say what? Did you know that everything wasn't for you? Tell that to my little bit younger self, and I would have been like, "If I have the time, then why not?"

When we are doing too much stuff, we consume ourselves with a bunch of undesired stuff, which in turn, leaves no room to hear from God in the needed stuff.

We can preoccupy ourselves even in serving that we miss out on the blessing.

When do you say no? You want to help, you have the time to help, but...

In the pause.

Every decision should be preceded by a pause. Every decision should cause you to evaluate your heart behind it.

If there is reservation, you go to God. If there is a decision, you also go to God. Discipline in making decisions is structure for you to have a confident walk with God.

Every decision needs to start with a pause. We need to obtain guidance for our decisions.

Let the wise hear and increase in learning, and the one who understands obtain guidance. Proverbs 1:5

Journal

Day 7

Take time to meditate on God's word. What's on your heart this week?

_____

_____

_____

_____

_____

_____

_____

_____

_____

_____

_____

_____

_____

_____

_____

_____

_____

_____

_____

_____

Week Forty

Day 1

DON'T BE INTIMIDATED BY THE PLAY

I watched as my boy played baseball one night. I saw the coaches at first and third. I saw the players all over the field covering their bases and guarding their positions, in stance and ready for the next play. Then I saw the other team's batter at home plate squaring up in the batter's box getting ready to hit the ball. I could imagine the intimidation. I could imagine the fear of striking out. I could imagine the desire to want to make a good hit. I could imagine the nerves being there. The only one standing up against all the others trying to hit the ball to the best of their ability as parents and teammates are zoned in on the next play.

Sometimes life can make us feel like the batter in the batter's box.

It's intimidating. It's scary. The nerves and stress begin to roll in. Sometimes we hit the ball out of the ballpark, and other times, we strike out. That baseball game reminded me of life.

God quickly reminded me of His love for me this morning. Have you ever felt like that player in the batter's box?

I'm here to remind you today that God has better plans than you can imagine for whatever you may be facing. I'm also speaking to myself.

No matter the play that is going to happen or already has,

Jesus already won the victory on the cross.

Today, celebrate the victory, and don't be intimidated by the play.

You've already won!

For everyone who has been born of God overcomes the world. And this is the victory that has overcome the world—our faith. Who is it that overcomes the world except the one who believes that Jesus is the Son of God? 1 John 5:4-5

Day 2

ABIDING IN HIS SHADOW

A shadow is a dark area where light is blocked by an opaque object. The cross section of a shadow is a two-dimensional silhouette, or a reverse projection of the object blocking the light.

What shadow we are allowing others to see? With what are we blocking the light of Jesus? I don't want to see my shadow, I want to be abiding and hiding under His.

The last part of that definition is a reverse projection of the object blocking the light. Just what if the only silhouette we and others saw when we looked at our shadow is of where we were blocking the light of Jesus? What areas in our lives could be blocking the light of Jesus?

Can you imagine, instead of seeing a silhouette of yourself in the light that is cast on the sidewalk, you saw a silhouette of just the part of yourself where you aren't allowing Jesus to truly shine through you - your eyes, your mouth, your ears, your hands, or maybe even just your heart?

This week I want us to take time to evaluate where we could be blocking Jesus from shining and make sure we are abiding in His shadow and not our own.

Keep me as the apple of your eye; hide me in the shadow of your wings.
Psalm 17:8

Day 3

FINE PRINT

I'm a big picture kind of girl. I like to know the big picture of what's going to happen. I like all the details, but sometimes I want to skip the fine print that a lot of people don't like to read. You know, the stuff at the bottom of commercials or a contract. Probably the most important stuff that needs to be read. Those warnings you just would rather skip over.

I tend to get that way in my walk with the Lord. You know what I'm saying? I want the final product or the big picture of what God's doing, but I don't want to go through the fine details He needs me to so I can get there. Sometimes I would like to skip the fine print because in the fine print, the words may scare me a little.

Warning God has something huge in store for you. More magnificent than you can imagine, and He is doing great things in you in the fine print. This is also where He is equipping and preparing you for that big picture you've been praying for. These details are important!

It's true, the fine print is where God will strengthen us and get us where we need to be for the bigger picture.

Trust in the process!

Is there something you are going through, and you feel like you're in that tiny print? Maybe it's not even clear, or it's hard to see the big picture right now. Put your trust in God through those tiny details. He is equipping, preparing, and

nourishing your heart. He has beautiful things in store for you.

Pure gold put in the fire comes out of it proved pure; genuine faith put through this suffering comes out proved genuine. When Jesus wraps this all up, it's your faith, not your gold, that God will have on display as evidence of his victory. 1 Peter 1:7

Day 4

WHO YOU ARE MEANT TO BE

What is self-pity?

Self-pity - a self-indulgent dwelling on one's own sorrows or misfortunes

Seems like a pretty easy equation to not get involved in. Self-pity equals the enemy, but for some reason, all of us at some point fall into the stage of self-pity.

The enemy lies to us about who we are and steals from us who we can be.

How true is that?

How many times do we allow the enemy to lie to us about who we are and then steal from us our purpose in the first place! Self-pity is destructive, just as the enemy himself is.

God tells you the truth about who you are so you can become who you are meant to be.

In those times of self-pity, change your outlook and reevaluate your perspective. Who we are meant to be is a child of God through Christ. One who is loved, adored, forgiven, and cherished.

In him we have redemption through his blood, the forgiveness of sins, in accordance with the riches of God's grace. Ephesians 1:7 (NIV)

Day 5

THE WILL OF GOD

What are we willing to sacrifice for the Lord?

The reality is that some days I feel like I could give a lot, and then some days, honestly, I wouldn't want to give up my last cookie with milk before bed. Seriously, there are days I get up, and I want to give God my all, every last part of me, but then something comes up and gets in the way of me wanting or actually doing it.

Whether it is time, energy, or just desire.

Sacrifice is huge. You are having to give up something. Can you imagine what Jesus felt going to the cross?

And going a little farther he fell on his face and prayed, saying, "My Father, if it be possible, let this cup pass from me; nevertheless, not as I will, but as you will."
Matthew 26:39

Jesus wanted the will of God. He knew what the will of God meant. He knew that sacrifice was dependent on the will of God.

For us sacrifice is also dependent on the will of God. A lot of times, it takes us giving up something we don't want to give up and taking that extra step; you know, the one we may not want to take.

It may be hard, but it's worth it! Jesus knew that the cup he had was hard, but He also knew that it was worth it. He

knew what step had to be taken in order for the will of God to be put in place.

What's your cup? What's God asking you to sacrifice today? Is it time? Is it a guilty pleasure you have? What's the first thing that comes to mind that you know God has been on your heart to sacrifice so that His will may be done in your life?

Everything I have ever sacrificed for God has been worth it! There has been no time, no energy, no self-satisfying pleasure, or no holding of my tongue that when I have given it to God, He hasn't satisfied my heart with more.

He is worth the sacrifice!

Day 6

THE NEW IS HERE

"Therefore, if anyone is in Christ, the new creation has come: The old
has gone, the new is here!"
2 Corinthians 5:17 (NIV)

A new creation is a process. When God created in Genesis, He didn't just create everything and say, "Boom, here it is." God first created the Heaven and earth. Then he created light, oceans, land, the sun and moon. When God creates a new work inside of us, we have to understand that it's a process. Just as He knew where to start with the creation around us, He knows exactly where to start inside of us.

When we become new in Him, He has to begin to purify and cleanse us from the inside out. He has created the inner most depth of us. With the same light that He shined onto darkness into creation, He shines inside of us under His new creations.

We are releasing the old us into the new we are becoming in Him.

"the new is here!"

Your old is gone and your new has arrived.

Do you believe that?

You are His new creation being refined and purified. Believe in His process today.

Journal

Day 7

Take time to meditate on God's word. What's on your heart this week?

_____

_____

_____

_____

_____

_____

_____

_____

_____

_____

_____

_____

_____

_____

_____

_____

_____

_____

Week Forty-One

Day 1

YIELD TO HIS AUTHORITY

How do we yield to His authority, His power, His control, and His possession?

One day as I was traveling the same road I do weekly to get to work, I passed a yield sign. I couldn't help but grin after all God did over the weekend at our 341 Invoke women's retreat and the reminder it put inside my heart, but even with that smile I realized this yield sign was different. I had never seen it before. It had just been put up. All I could do was thank Him, not just for the sweet reminder, but for also putting a new sweet sound of peace inside of me.

Truly, His mercies are new EVERY morning.

Did you know the yield sign actually means that you don't have the right of way?

I know someone that does, though. Someone who is always sufficient, always knowing, and always giving.

That leaves me with.....

Are you yielding to your Father?

Take time when you are in fear, in doubt, in worry, or in turmoil to yield to His presence, His power, and His control. Take time today in the "even if's," "what if's" or just the consuming busyness, to yield to God.

Pause and allow Him to direct your steps. Allow Him to

position you exactly where He needs you.

Trust in the Lord with all your heart, and do not lean on your own understanding. In all your ways acknowledge him, and he will make straight your paths.
Proverbs 3:5-6

Day 2

FEELING OF LONLINESS

Have you ever been lonely? Loneliness comes in many forms. It could be that you are going through something, and you feel like you have no one. It could be that you have moved away and feel like you are miles away from others. It could just be that empty feeling of not being in a relationship with Jesus and needing something more. The enemy loves to make us feel like we are all alone, and he loves to do that because when he starts to make us feel like we are alone, he can then begin to get inside our minds. When he starts to get inside our minds, we start to not just think we are lonely, but we start to think a million other things, and the unintended thoughts of the enemy take the forefront over God's truth.

I think of when Peter was put into prison; the feeling of loneliness that must have come over him. You know that feeling that makes us ask, "God, where are you?"

And behold, an angel of the Lord stood next to him, and a light shone in the cell. He struck Peter on the side and woke him, saying, "Get up quickly." And the chains fell off his hands. Acts 12:7

When you start to feel alone, I think this is a huge reminder of what we must do. GET UP QUICKLY. The enemy's intentions for our loneliness only restrict us from God's glory in our greatness.

If you're lonely, get up. Know that you have others praying for you. Get yourself into a group that can love on you and instill the truth of the word inside of you. God never intended us to do life alone or to feel lonely.

Day 3

SEATED AT HIS TABLE

Have you ever imagined the dinner table at the last supper? We don't know much of what was there, but we do know those details that are important for us to remember. It doesn't talk about the food or the decorations. It tells us a story of significance.

The significance of that meal often goes through my mind during gatherings. The fact that Jesus knew that someone who was joining Him for His last meal would betray Him. The fact that Jesus still offered forgiveness at His last supper before His arrest and crucifixion. The fact that Jesus was always serving others. He is the example of who we should be.

Now as they were eating, Jesus took bread, and after blessing it broke it and gave it to the disciples, and said, "Take and eat; this is my body." And he took a cup, and when He had given thanks he gave it to them, saying, "Drink of it, all of you, for this is my blood of the covenant, which is poured out for many for the forgiveness of sins."
Matthew 26:26-28

Three words jumped out at me when I read these verses:

"All of you." Knowing that as He sat there, all of them were still offered the forgiveness of the Father no matter what one of them was about to do. This story is such a reminder to me that no matter where we all find ourselves, He is always offering us a seat at His table to drink from His cup, and we can be filled!

Day 4

CRAVE A RELATIONSHIP

How much does He have to do before we stop allowing ourselves to doubt, and we just begin to believe who He is?

Hearing from God is vital in our walk with God! What keeps us alive? Food and water are some of the necessities for us to live. Some may be insulin dependent; others rely on other medications to keep them well. There are things that we must do to keep us alive. They're vital for our health. I know that if I don't eat, after a while I start getting hangry (hungry and angry put together), and everyone had better watch out.

We need to see a relationship with God as vital.

We need to start realizing that his presence is needed every day, not just when we feel like we need him. We must seek His direction like He seeks our attention.

When we go to God and ask Him for things, we shouldn't just be takers. Who likes to have a friend who only comes to us when they need something? God wants to be our friend and our Father. He wants to be our everything, but for that to be possible, we need to know about Him. We can't just tell Him everything about ourselves and about our needs and not learn about Him in return. To be honest, He already knows all those things but still chooses to listen.

"I am the vine; you are the branches. Whoever abides in me and I in him, it is that bears much fruit, for apart from me you can do nothing." John 15:5

We need Him. We can try to figure it out and do it our own way, but eventually we will fall. When we do, we will cry out for His help.

Let's love Him like He's our everything. That way, when we do need Him, and we will, He will know we aren't just coming with needs, we are coming with love. He will know that we crave a relationship, not just someone to fulfill our needs.

Day 5

IN THE MIDDLE

By faith, Noah built a ship in the middle of dry land.
Hebrews 11:7 (MSG)

I read that scripture and had one of those, "Okay, God" moments. "I hear you speaking to me," and as if the word pruning didn't do anything, I heard loud and clear, "In the middle."

In the middle of dry land, Noah built his ship. In the middle, where we seem so defeated and there doesn't seem like a way out, God is building something through us. Noah didn't build His ship near the ocean. Actually, I don't think there was an ocean anywhere in sight from where Noah built his ship, but Noah trusted God. By faith, Noah did what God was instructing him to do, and even in the middle, Noah was obedient.

The middle is important!

Can we be obedient and trust God even "in the middle?"

In the middle is the central location where God is working on our hearts.

Day 6

BEFORE THE HEALING TAKES PLACE

Have you ever been physically wounded? If you have, you know that a wound has a process that it has to go through in order for it to heal. I can remember when I was younger flipping a four-wheeler. I had scabs, bruises, and couldn't use my right leg for some time. It took almost a week before I could begin to walk normally again. There aren't any external scars left of those injuries, but I will always remember that day. I can also remember a time falling on a go kart muffler trying to push it up the hill. I had severe burns on the inside of my leg. Again, no physical scars were left, but that memory will forever be inscribed in my mind. I do have a scar, however, from a cheer incident where my friend's chin collided with my eyebrow and ripped it open, and I had to have stitches. There will always be a scar above my right eye that will be a reminder of that day.

No wound isn't opened before it's healed.

The wounds that are deep inside of us, the emotional wounds, have a process just as the physical ones. They also must be opened before the healing takes place. God didn't intend for wounds to stay open. He intended for a process through Him to bring healing inside of us.

With a physical wound, we have no idea what the process is going to look like. We can assume, but it could take months for something to fully heal back to the same as before. Other times, we are left with the reminder in a

scar. With internal wounds, emotional wounds, it's the same. It takes time for God to work inside of us. It takes time for healing. The Bible says,

> *We are pressed on every side by troubles, but we are not crushed. We are perplexed, but not driven to despair.*
> *2 Corinthians 4:8 (NLT)*

If you read the same full scripture in The Message it says this,

> *We've been surrounded and battered by troubles, but we're not demoralized; we're not sure what to do, but we know that God knows what to do; we've been spiritually terrorized, but God hasn't left our side; we've been thrown down, but we haven't broken. What they did to Jesus, they do to us—trial and torture, mockery and murder; what Jesus did among them, he does in us—he lives! Our lives are at constant risk for Jesus' sake, which makes Jesus' life all the more evident in us. While we're going through the worst, you're getting in on the best! 2 Corinthians 4:8-18 (MSG)*

What a promise for us to remember - God is making us new again! He is healing and restoring our wounds. He is alive in us, making new creations through us.

"While we're going through the worst, you're getting in on the best."

Journal

Day 7

Take time to meditate on God's word. What's on your heart this week?

_____

_____

_____

_____

_____

_____

_____

_____

_____

_____

_____

_____

_____

_____

_____

_____

_____

_____

_____

_____

_____

_____

Week Forty-Two

Day 1

SHOW HIM YOUR LOVE

Our hearts should be set on doing the things we do because we love the Lord. He supplies when we are in need. He comforts us when we are down. He strengthens us when we need strength. He is such a good Father. Always there, always near, and always ready to pick us up. Some things we can do to thank Him and to let him know we love Him:

- Praise Him: Rejoice, sing praises. The Bible tells us to come into His presence with singing. Let the Holy Spirit move you so that you may embrace God's goodness.

- Serve: Give back what God gives to you. God wants us all to have servants' hearts.

- Know Him: We can say we love Him, but do we really know Him? Study your Bible; seek Him in all you do. Become friends with the Lord. Just as you know about the people who are in your life, you should know even more about your Heavenly Father.

- Thank Him: Remember to always give thanks for who He is, what He has done, and what we know He will do.

It's so easy for us to say we love the Lord, but we really need to show Him we love Him with our actions and with our hearts.

Jesus replied: "'Love the Lord your God with all your heart and with all your soul and with all your mind.' Matthew 22:37 (NIV)

Day 2

SURFACE LEVEL

A lot of times we tend to look at things from the surface level of emotions.

For instance, this person hurt me, and this is how I feel, so in return this is how I will react. God didn't intend for our hearts to be surface level, and he didn't intend for us to live a surface level life. We have to be careful what we are allowing to flow from our hearts.

If you look deeper into how God structured our hearts, you'll see that the vessels in the heart bring oxygen-free blood into the heart and then oxygen-rich blood back out. In the same way, we can bring nothing rich into the heart, but God produces what's rich inside the heart and then sends it back out.

God is what oxygenates us. He is our source, and in order to stop living surface level we must not only guard our hearts, but we must also realize that life is meant for much more than just surface level thinking. God has intended us to live a much deeper life.

Let's make sure we are allowing the flow from our hearts to be from Him filled with His oxygen that we can share with others.

Above all else, guard your heart, for everything you do flows from it.
Proverbs 4:23 (NIV)

Day 3

STAY DETERMINED

Have you ever had to persevere through a trial?

Persistence means to do something despite difficulty or delay in achieving success. It's staying determined and having tenacity.

The parable of the persistent widow:

And he told them a parable to the effect that they ought always to pray and not lose heart. He said, "In a certain city there was a judge who neither feared God nor respected man. And there was a widow in that city who kept coming to him and saying, 'Give me justice against my adversary.' For a while he refused, but afterward he said to himself, 'Though I neither fear God nor respect man, yet because this widow keeps bothering me, I will give her justice, so that she will not beat me down by her continual coming.'" And the Lord said, "Hear what the unrighteous judge says. And will not God give justice to his elect, who cry to him day and night? Will he delay long over them? I tell you, he will give justice to them speedily. Nevertheless, when the Son of Man comes, will he find faith on earth?"
Luke 18:1-8

Two main details you can point out from this parable is that Jesus says to:

1. Always Pray
2. Don't lose heart

Having a consistent prayer life is important, and when we aren't hearing from God, remaining steadfast in that is even

more important. Just because you aren't hearing doesn't mean He isn't working!

What does it mean to lose heart? Losing heart means to lose hope of where you've come from. We need to remember where we've come from so we can remember where we are going. Not dwelling on the past and keeping our eyes on the present and the future but remembering that God has brought us far.

Jesus is giving a promise of who God is in this parable and what He will do.

When we remain persistent, He always prevails!

Day 4

TENDING THE SHEEP

Even though I walk through the valley of the shadow of death, I will fear no evil, for you are with me; your rod and your staff, they comfort me. Psalm 23:4

In this passage the Lord is referred to as our shepherd and we are His sheep. When shepherds herd sheep, they use a rod or staff to protect them from any animals that may come near to them and hurt them as they are walking. They also use it to keep them on the path, to comfort them when they have strayed, and to let them know the shepherd is still there.

When times seem tough and we have more than we can bear, we should feel comforted knowing God is near. He is our shepherd through the valleys. He walks with us, tends to us, comforts us, and protects us. In our darkest days He is always there to direct our paths. Don't fear your situation, but instead find hope within it that the Lord is your resting place. You can find rest within Him as He is always there to be your security through your deepest valleys.

Day 5

SOLID FOUNDATION

Love is, patient, love is kind. It does not envy, it does not boast, it is not proud. It does not dishonor others, it is not self-seeking, it is not easily angered, it keeps no records of wrongs. Love does not delight in evil but rejoices in truth. It always protects, always trusts, always hopes and always perseveres. Love never fails.
1 Corinthians 13:4-8 (NIV)

In marriage God comes first, and your spouse comes second. For them to take the place right under God in the way you love is huge. When two become one, you both put yourselves in that place together. Right under the hand of God. We have to learn, then, to love beyond limits as we love ourselves.

Marriage isn't easy, but God always has a purpose and plan for everything.

When going into a marriage you need to start with a solid foundation. We need to have a foundation set on God.

Wives, submit yourselves to your husbands, as is fitting in the Lord. Husbands, love your wives, and do not be harsh with them.
Colossians 3:18-19

It also speaks on the same thing in Ephesians 5:22-33

When wives submit to their husbands, it's not making them any less of a woman, it's allowing them to love as Christ loves us. God wants us to submit to our husbands out of our love for Christ. We are to humble ourselves and allow God to lead our relationships. It says, "submit as it is fitting

to the Lord." The Lord wants us to love them as we do Him.

This is what the Lord has called to be our first jobs. To honor and take care of them. He gave us marriage, and He gave us love.

Building a marriage on a foundation of Christ gives you the power of hope. When we can learn to love as Christ has loved us, we can share with them our love for Christ. We can also learn sacrifice and dedication.

God gave us our spouse. Put God first and allow your marriage to grow on the love you have for the Lord.

Day 6

UNDER PRESSURE

Ever thought about how a pressure cooker works? It's a pot that's controlled with a valve, and as the pressure increases or builds inside of it, the pot heats. Then the liquid insides heats to form steam which, in turn, causes your food to cook faster and to be more tender.

Have you ever felt yourself under a lot of pressure? The pressure where the heat is on, but goodness, nothing feels like it's cooking. You actually feel quite the opposite.

Think of it like this. You are the pressure cooker. God's controlling the valve to get all those things inside you right, so He can use you where He needs you. Sometimes the heat may be turned up, and the enemy wants you to think you're burning, but the reality is that you're just going to come out more tender and perfect. God's in control of that valve! Who can really say that they've thought, "Turn up the heat, God!"?

Not me, I'm probably more like, "Lord, I need you to turn down the heat." He knows our limitations, though. If you're under pressure or feeling the heat of life today, remember God is a sovereign God. What the enemy is trying to make you think will destroy you, God's using to tenderize you.

For you know that the testing of your faith produces steadfastness.
And let the steadfastness have its full effect, that you may be perfect
and complete, lacking in nothing. James 1:3-4

Journal

Day 7

Take time to meditate on God's word. What's on your heart this week?

_____

_____

_____

_____

_____

_____

_____

_____

_____

_____

_____

_____

_____

_____

_____

_____

_____

_____

Week Forty-Three

Day 1

HINDERANCE OF PRIDE

Being prideful is not something God wants of us. We can have too much pride at times - we don't apologize when we know we are in the wrong, or we have too much pride to turn the other cheek. I think the one a lot of us fall into is being too prideful to say, "I'm sorry" first, even though we know the other person may be wrong.

God wants us to humble ourselves. He wants us to be able to take our pride in situations and cover it with humility. Jesus, who was perfect, was able to humble Himself and wash his disciples' feet in John 13:1-17.

"Truly, truly, I say to you, a servant is not greater than his master, nor is a messenger greater than the one who sent him. If you know these things, blessed are you if you do them." John 13:16-17

We can sometimes be too prideful in our actions. We forget why and who we are here for. It's not about what we have or what we've done. Pride can be a wall between you and God.

In his pride the wicked man does not seek him; in all his thoughts there is no room for God.
Psalms 10:4 (NIV)

Pride sometimes can hinder one's thoughts, but God wants you to humble yourself before Him to be who He calls you to be. All the glory here today and forever belongs to Him! Do not be too prideful in your ways. Acknowledge your sin and be reminded that you are nothing compared to what God is prepared to do through you.

Day 2

TEAR DOWN THE WALLS

Through the years we go through things that make us build walls. These walls can represent many different feelings we go through, and we continue to add stones, one after one, until we shut ourselves down in certain areas. This can cause a wall that blocks us from seeing what God may want us to see.

Sometimes building these walls makes us feel good because we feel like we are protecting ourselves from being hurt again, but God wants us to not be afraid. I read a statement one time that said, "build bridges not walls."

God doesn't want us to shut ourselves down from potentially receiving what He has in store for us. When we do that, we are losing out on what God may have for us to help us grow. God wants us to be equipped and armored, ready to approach any situation. He wants us to be fully in the word and in prayer so that we don't need a wall because He has become our defense. He wants us ready to welcome things across our bridge, prepared and knowing,

Walls can allow us to miss our God-given potential. Walls can be fear, anxiousness, and deceit; but a bridge is welcoming, wisdom, and growth. Don't miss out on what God has for you by hiding behind the wall!

"Have I not commanded you? Be strong and courageous. Do not be afraid; do not be discouraged, for the Lord your God will be with you wherever you go." Joshua 1:9 (NIV)

Day 3

HERE COMES THAT DREAMER

Jealousy, envy, temptation, and deceit started early on in Genesis. Joseph is someone that had a calling on his life, but others were envious. Joseph knew God was calling Him. He started having visions of himself being in a higher position, and he told his brothers about those visions; however, because of sin (jealousy and envy), he ended up finding himself in trouble.

Sometimes what God tells us isn't for everyone else. Pray before seeking wisdom from others. Sometimes what God gives you in prayer or vision may need to be just between you and God before He brings it to fruition.

They said to one another, "Here comes this dreamer."
Genesis 37:19

They threw him into a pit before selling him to the Ishmaelites. Little did they know that Joseph's dream would still become reality because He was following God's calling upon His life.

When God has placed His hand on your life to do something, no matter the obstacles or adversity you may face, God's plans will always prevail.

God knew that envy and jealousy would come against Joseph. He also knew the lies and deceit that would come. God knows what will come at you as well. This insight should help you to keep going. Trials may come, but it always comes back to God. Step into His presence, and step into your calling no matter what you may face. God

uses all things together for your good. He will turn things around to teach you and make you wise in His ways.

Keep following God's calling upon your life despite the setbacks.

Day 4

GENERATIONAL CHANGE

Generational change has been something on my heart for a while. A change that you make inside your own walls, including your own heart, that is then instilled inside your homes. A change that not only your children take with them to their children but change that exists for generations to come.

How do we make generational change when we are a product of our own generation? I'm so glad you asked!

Generational change causes us to step out into the boldness God intended for us. It causes us to change things inside our homes and our hearts that have been planted for many generations.

Think about it, if we don't show our children courageousness in the right forms, they'll learn it in the worldly ones. If we don't put Biblical transformation inside our homes through what the word says, our kids will be transformed by what people say.

This starts inside of us! If we don't start with change planted on the foundation of God, we will continue to be only products of our generation. We are more than products; we are the change!

Generational change starts today. Every day is a new day to begin to make a bold change into what God has called over our families. Every day as we take confident steps into God's plan, we take bold and courageous steps into changing our hearts and the many generations to come. It's

never too late to start a generational impact!

Start with prayer inside your homes and devotionals with your children. Center the foundation around Him.

One generation shall commend your works to another, and shall declare your mighty acts. Psalm 145:4

Day 5

DON'T MISS OUT
ON THE PRESENT

Don't we live in a time where there is so much to distract us? I find myself distracted not just by my phone or tv, but by my thoughts about yesterday or tomorrow, and I forget to be in the present.

I can remember sharing a conversation with someone one day, and at the end of it realizing I didn't remember anything that they had just said. That honestly hurt my heart that someone was displaying theirs, and I was so distracted by other things that I couldn't put myself in the now.

I can also remember a time that the same thing happened to me. As I shared my heart, I remember feeling disconnected. The person seemed mentally preoccupied, and it made me feel as if they really didn't care.

Don't we all sometimes fight with truly being in the present and end up missing out on so many important opportunities placed in our paths?

I think about the significant prayer request I missed out on, or the deeper connection to someone's heart that I failed to have.

We shouldn't want to miss out on the present opportunity to show God's love. These sweet appointments created by Him have been created for us to be able to help someone in their now. Let's remember to show our complete devotion

to God by giving our undivided attention to others when
He places them in our paths.

*I am saying this for your benefit, not to place restrictions on you. I
want you to do whatever will help you serve the Lord best, with as few
distractions as possible.*
1 Corinthians 7:35 (NLT)

Day 6

KEEP GOING

We do a lot based off emotions - the way we respond to someone or the way we handle a situation; we could probably make a long list of specific instances when we use our emotions to determine our words and actions.

Reading through Acts, one of the things I've realized is that even then there was so much that could discourage them from spreading the Gospel or walking with the Lord. Even they got discouraged, but they chose to keep going.

We are going to have emotions. We are going to feel sad, angry, upset, tired, bitter, guilty, or just downright in a funk sometimes.

It's not about the emotions as much as what we choose to do with them.

For we do not want you to be unaware, brothers, of the affliction we experienced in Asia. For we were so utterly burdened beyond our strength that we despaired of life itself. Indeed, we felt that we had received the sentence of death. But that was to make us rely not on ourselves but on God who raises the dead. He delivered us from such a deadly peril, and he will deliver us. On him we have set our hope that he will deliver us again. 2 Corinthians 1:8-10

Paul knew that he was utterly burdened beyond his strength. He also knew what he needed to do with that emotion of despair. He had to fully rely on God, but he also knew that, when we lack hope, we also lack the emotions that go with it! He had to put his hope in the Lord that He would deliver them again. He chose to

have hope! What emotion have you been choosing over having hope?

Are you burdened beyond your strength? Put your hope in God today!

Journal

Day 7

Take time to meditate on God's word. What's on your heart this week?

_____

_____

_____

_____

_____

_____

_____

_____

_____

_____

_____

_____

_____

_____

_____

_____

_____

_____

_____

Week Forty-Four

Day 1

GIVE NO ROOM

There are times when we may not realize it, but we are giving room for the devil to come in.

Be angry and do not sin; do not let the sun go down on your anger, and give no opportunity to the devil.
Ephesians 4:26-27

When we are upset, God wants us to come to Him right away with our frustrations. When we wait, we allow ourselves to start harboring negative feelings that can lead to negative thoughts. This, in turn, allows more room for the devil to enter. We begin to dwell on things that are not of God. Think about it — if every time someone frustrated us we immediately took five minutes to pray about it, we would begin to process it and let it go. God then begins to take it over and use it for good.

When something frustrating happens, we can tend to call on the wrong people. We talk to friends and vent, or we even go to the source. Then we amp ourselves up from the feedback and become more bitter.

God doesn't give us feelings of bitterness or frustration. God desires healing and restoration.

The next time someone begins to work their way under your nerves, take a few minutes and pray before you run to the wrong person. Don't give the devil any room to come in. Shut him down and shut him out.

Day 2

GO THE DISTANCE

To what length would you go for your relationship with God?

It's easy for us to say, "I'd go the distance. Whatever length He may take me, or I would need to go," but the reality is that in that distance we become weary and tired.

I have been thinking of the lengths we go to for our families and our friends. The lengths we go to, to make sure those we love are taken care of. Are we truly going the same lengths to make sure our relationship with God is taken care of?

I know I would go to the ends of this earth for my family, for my friends, and for those God puts into my path to love. God wants that. He wants our ministry to be in our homes, in our churches, and in our hearts as we walk around day to day, but He wants, first and foremost, the depths of our hearts to be with Him.

That got me to thinking. What lengths am I going to for Him? What depth of pain would I experience for Him? What time and sacrifice do I give to Him? He has gone the distance for us. Will we go the distance for Him?

I appeal to you therefore, brothers, by the mercies of God, to present your bodies as a living sacrifice, holy and acceptable to God, which is your spiritual worship.
Romans 12:1

Day 3

EVERY

Have you ever gotten a word stuck in your head and just couldn't seem to shake it? That's what happened with the word "every" for me. Did you know that one definition of the word "every" is "all possible, utmost"?

The word "every" has been on my heart so much lately. As I think of the word, I think of everything that God has done for me and everything I want to be. God is our every!

Everything
Everywhere
Every way

He is the all possible and the utmost! As we strive to work on who we are every day, our God is everything we strive to be.

Listen to God's voice in everything you do, everywhere you go; he's the one who will keep you on track.
Proverbs 3:6 (MSG)

Everything is needed for our growth with God, and nothing is insignificant. Every day is important, and everything belongs to Him.

Today look at the BIG picture of everything. Who is the BIG picture over your situation or circumstance that may be everything to you right now? Take time to listen for His voice. He is every, He is all possible.

Day 4

DAY OF BREAKTHROUGH

Today is the day of breakthrough. This is so easy to write but may not be as easy to believe.

Have you ever said, "It's going to happen today? I'm going to get that breakthrough," and then as the night comes, you realize, nope, it didn't come today?

I think we all find ourselves in desperate places like that searching for that breakthrough.

What do we do even when it's not today?

Well I've been known to kick, scream, yell, fuss, and fight back with God. Wondering why He hadn't shown up and then sitting there afterward realizing that I still hadn't heard from Him, but now I just feel awful for being so hateful.

It's hard when you are in the waiting period of hearing something from the Lord. However, I'm always reminded that even in the crushing the Lord is making something "new." Something that has to happen.

So many people in the Bible found themselves in a crushing period from the beginning to the end, even Jesus. One of his own disciples betrayed Him. Jesus may have known this was going to happen but think about how crushing it must have been to know someone He loved and trusted would hurt Him.

We are not exempt from the crushing periods, but what we do in the "even when" matters.

We are afflicted in every way, but not crushed; perplexed, but not driven to despair; persecuted, but not forsaken; struck down, but not destroyed; 2 Corinthians 4:8-9

Maybe you've been waiting for years, but even when you don't get your answer today, be reminded that in the crushing you are being made new, because with Jesus "WE WILL NOT BE DESTROYED!"

Day 5

PIECES

How do you begin to pick up the pieces,
when your world comes crashing down?

Where do you look to find the answers,
when the answers can't seem to be found?

When fear sneaks his ugly face
through the crack of weakness that he found.

The light may seem so distant,
but the truth is God is all around.

When we lift our eyes to heaven
and begin to see his grace.

The light begins to look closer
because it never left shining in our place.

You see weakness may seem like defeat
straight from the enemy.

But weakness is truly a plea
that sends us to our knees.

Your pieces may seem like they are broken
shattered or incomplete

But, the one who said it is finished
will meet you at mercy's seat.

Let His face rest upon you,

let your night turn into day.

His power is made perfect in our weakness.
He will never fail us, and He will always make a way.

This is a poem I wrote as we were going through a tragic and unexpected death through suicide in my husband's family. We were trying to pick up the pieces that were scattered all around us. Through the therapy of a piece of paper and pen I was able to process those pieces. If you have pieces you are trying to pick up today or piece back together, I hope this poem will help you to remember how perfect His power is made through our weakness. I also want you to remember you are never alone!

But he said to me, "My grace is sufficient for you, for my power is made perfect in weakness." Therefore I will boast all the more gladly of my weaknesses, so that the power of Christ may rest upon me.
2 Corinthians 12:9

Day 6

BEWARE OF FALSE PROPHETS

There will be people in the world and even in church that will give you the wrong information from the Bible. They put on an outward appearance of wisdom but on the inside do not know truth. The Bible tells us to be aware and watch out for these people.

> *"Beware of false prophets, who come to you in sheep's clothing but inwardly are ravenous wolves."*
> *Matthew 7:15*

The Bible tells us that we will recognize these people by their fruits; their lack of knowledge will be known.

This is a prime example of why we must take the time to spend with God and read the Bible ourselves.

The scripture tells us to beware, so we are not filling ourselves or others with something not of God.

Journal

Day 7

Take time to meditate on God's word. What's on your heart this week?

_____

_____

_____

_____

_____

_____

_____

_____

_____

_____

_____

_____

_____

_____

_____

_____

_____

_____

Week Forty-Five

Day 1

WHAT'S YOUR CONTRIBUTION?

We read in Mark the greatest commandments.

"And to love him with all the heart and with all the understanding and with all the strength, and to love one's neighbor as oneself, is much more than all whole burnt offerings and sacrifices."
Mark 12:33

When you scroll down and read a little farther, you will read about a widow who offered everything she had.

It made me begin to question how much I am contributing to the kingdom of heaven.

"For they all contributed out of their abundance, but she out of her poverty has put in everything she had, all she has to live on."
Mark 12:44

It's easy to contribute from abundance. The widow's heart wasn't set on herself. Her abundance didn't come from what she had that others could see. Her abundance came from what was inside of her. Her heart was set on the Kingdom.

Lord, I pray our hearts are set on the Kingdom and not on what others can see. I pray that today and every day You open us up to be an abundant giver. To contribute to Your Kingdom not from what we have but from our hearts. Knowing that when we love You with our all we give our all to those around us.

Day 2

GO AWAY WITH ME

I think God just wants us to go away with Him. Something life-giving happens when I get alone with Him. So many times, in the Bible Jesus goes alone to a place to pray. In Mark we see that His disciples were going with Him spreading His word of repentance, and He tells them to go alone and rest awhile.

And he said to them, "Come away by yourselves to a desolate place and rest awhile." Mark 6:31

I used to never like to be by myself; I always felt like I needed someone. It's funny how we always consume ourselves with unneeded things when we are bored or have a little downtime. I realize now that I was truly just lacking a relationship with God. I had what I needed right at my fingertips.

I realize that taking care of me means that I need time alone with the One who matters most. It's not for selfish ambition, but it's for the desires of my heart to be replenished in His spirit and for His will over my life.

When is the last time you just went away with Him? Sometimes getting alone with Him in an isolated place is just what your heart needs.

Today I challenge you to find a place. Somewhere empty and talk to Him. See just how He replenishes your spirit and mind this week.

Day 3

THE LAST DAYS

But understand this, that in the last days there will come times of difficulty. For people will be lovers of self, lovers of money, proud, arrogant, abusive, disobedient to their parents, ungrateful, unholy, heartless, unappeasable, slanderous, without self-control, brutal, not loving good, **treacherous***, reckless, swollen with conceit, lovers of pleasure rather than lovers of God, having the appearance of godliness, but denying its power. Avoid such people.*
2 Timothy 3:1-5

We are to avoid these people. God tells us that these people will lead us astray, and we may never know the truth.

Let's not be an imposter in our faith. Let's make our love for Jesus Christ known. God knows our hearts, and we must be steadfast in our love for the Lord for all to see.

We need to pray that the Lord removes things that are not of Him so that others can see Him in us.

Prayer: God please make us less of the world and more of You. Please help us to love and show the love You have created in us. Thank You, Lord, for loving us enough that You went through so many persecutions and sufferings so that we could have everlasting life. Amen.

Day 4

PUT YOUR FATIH IN HIM

Jesus performed many miracles in the Bible.

And behold, some people brought to him a paralytic, lying on a bed. And when Jesus saw their faith, he said to the paralytic, "Take heart, my son; your sins are forgiven."
Matthew 9:2

"When Jesus saw their faith…" This phrase really stuck out to me. Jesus performs miracles when he sees our faith. You know Jesus knows our every thought. He knows what we believe and what we doubt. He knows if we are of little faith or if we believe that He is a miracle worker. He is all-knowing and all-powerful.

Can you think of something that you've been doubting or saying there is no hope in? My question for you to think about today is, "Where is your faith?"

Can Jesus see your faith in Him, or are you doubting Him in your situation?

Jesus said to the paralytic, "Take heart…"

Today take heart in where you are, believing in the miracle to come. He wants to see your faith in Him!

Day 5

PICK A DOOR

Which gate are you going through?

"Enter by the narrow gate. For the gate is wide and the way is easy that leads to destruction, and those who enter by it are many. For the gate is narrow and the way is hard that leads to life, and those who find it are few."
Matthew 7:13-14

If you were to see two doors, one with a wide entrance and one with a narrow one, which would you choose? Normally, we would probably say the wide gate just because it's easier to get through. In the scripture here it tells us that the wide gate is easy, but it leads to destruction. Okay, now if we knew that, we would have chosen the other gate. The narrow one leads to life.

This seems a lot like our own life. How many times have I probably chosen the wider gate? The gate that leads to destruction. I don't know about you, but honestly, probably too many to even count.

Just a pause, aren't you thankful for a forgiving God!

Now, I realize why it's so hard to walk through the narrow gate that leads to life. Following Jesus isn't a walk in the park. Coming to Jesus is easy. Following Jesus is hard.

Jesus wants us to live out the will of God in our lives. Doing that doesn't always come easy, but it will always come bringing life. Which gate are you choosing?

Day 6

THROUGH HIS EYES

The Bible talks about visions, and it even refers to our eyes.

"The eye is the lamp of the body. So, if your eye is healthy, your whole body will be full of light, but if your eye is bad, your whole body will be full of darkness."
Matthew 6:22-23

I found that research has even shown a totally blind person can sometimes still perceive light.

This made me think about the light my own eyes are perceiving.

When we lean into the world and away from Christ, that is when the light becomes dim or even sometimes nonexistent. Just as in the song, "Amazing Grace," the lyrics say, "I once was blind, but now I see." What are we seeing with our eyes?

Have you accepted Christ but still have a love for money? Have you given your life over to Him but still live the way you want?

Once we say, "God, we receive you," we are to take those blinders off and live in the fullness that He has created for us. When our eyes are healed, our whole body is full of light! God has intended you to see things in His vibrant light. Are you perceiving the light of God or the light of this world? Are your eyes healthy?

Journal

Day 7

Take time to meditate on God's word. What's on your
heart this week?

_____

_____

_____

_____

_____

_____

_____

_____

_____

_____

_____

_____

_____

_____

_____

_____

_____

_____

_____

Week Forty-Six

Day 1

I AM WHO I AM

I used to be the worst at saying this. I just am who I am, which I have found over the years is not true at all. I am who I am because I choose to be that way. I am who I am in Christ, and that's the choice we get to make.

We want people to look at us and say we are who we are because we are a child of The One True King. The way we present ourselves, the way we pray, and the way that Christ shines through us. We need to invest in what God has put right in front of us; walking in our season where God has us.

Some of the greatest callings begin with a very simple response. It doesn't take drastic things to get into His presence. Simple responses lead to extraordinary moves of God.

Now you are the body of Christ and individually members of it.
1 Corinthians 12:27

Day 2

GUARD YOUR TONGUE

Many times, the Bible talks about how we should be careful with our tongues. We need to be careful with what we say and how we say it.

Our words need to be Godly words from our hearts and not of the world. Sometimes when we express ourselves, we use a tone of voice, or we even say things we don't mean. We have to guard our words.

We need to communicate our feelings while making sure it's in a loving way. Our tongues can be like swords. They can be hurtful and leave lasting wounds on those we love. God said we should be slow to speak. This means we need to take time and think of the things we are going to say before we say them. What we say leaves lasting impacts on those around us.

Remember today as you speak, to speak love. If you are having trouble with the right words, stop and take a second to ask God to give you words of wisdom.

Let your speech always be gracious, seasoned with salt, so that you may know how you ought to answer each person.
Colossians 4:6

Day 3

THE EYE OF THE LORD

Behold, the eye of the Lord is on those who fear him, on those who hope in his steadfast love. Psalm 33:18

I never understood this statement until recently. Have you ever read something in the Bible, and you have no idea what it means? I always wondered why I should fear the Lord. I thought, "I don't want to be afraid of Him." Fearing the Lord, though, means so much more than that.

Fearing the Lord means that when you know something in your heart is not right, and when you feel the conviction of sin, instead of continuing in your sin, you choose God. We should fear the bad that can come from not listening to the Holy Spirit.

Fearing the Lord is having a relationship with Him and wanting to do what's right despite the world telling you to do differently.

Fearing God is knowing He is enough. The eye of the Lord is upon us.

Day 4

SLOW DOWN AND BEGIN

Sometimes we get so caught up in life that we forget that God only wants us to slow down and begin.

I have been called by name,
to do your great plan.

I need to concentrate on that,
and not of the world directed by man.

Lord, you are the purest of pure,
with a love like no other.

When you begin to shine through me,
I don't have to worry with trouble.

I know that your word is the highest of high.

So, whatever may come my way,
you have already healed and taken away.

Seeking you I will find peace, joy, and a love with no end.

All I need to do is slow down and begin.

For we are his workmanship, created in Christ Jesus for good works, which God prepared beforehand, that we should walk in them.
Ephesians 2:10

Day 5

IT DOESN'T MATTER

God is the same to everyone. It doesn't matter about color, sex, or race. It doesn't matter about past, future, or hate. God is love. He continues to let the sun rise and set. He continues to let storms come and pass.

He wants us to love the same as He does. He wants us to pray for our country and leaders. He wants us to push together and not pull apart. God says to love those who persecute you.

How do we love those who mean harm to us? In a world dwindling in faith, we are supposed to come together in the love of Christ. God works all things together for our good. The devil may work overtime to push people's hearts to kill, steal, and destroy, but God can overcome it. He can take those people and make them new in Him. He can work on their hearts just as He has worked on ours.

He died for the sinner!

We should want to see our nation come together. Love conquers all.

"But I say to you, Love your enemies and pray for those who persecute you, so that you may be sons of your Father who is in heaven. For he makes his sun rise on the evil and on the good, and sends rain on the just and on the unjust."
Matthew 5:44-45

Day 6

PRESSED DOWN

"Judge not, and you will not be judged; condemn not, and you will not be condemned; forgive, and you will be forgiven; give, and it will be given to you. Good measure, pressed down, shaken together, running over, will be put into your lap. For with the measure you use it will be measured back to you."
Luke 6:37-38

What should we do? Judge not, condemn not, forgive, and give. I am guilty of not always doing these things. What about you? I'm guilty of judging someone's character or reasoning. I am guilty of condemning someone for what they may have done wrong or how they may be living.

In reality these things should not affect me or you. Someone's bad attitude, someone's intentions, and someone's actions in no way affect us. We shouldn't allow ourselves to get so wrapped up in such a way that it makes us judge or condemn. Their way of living doesn't have anything to do with our quality of life besides the sin we choose to commit in focusing on what we have no control over.

Let's quit getting wrapped up in the things that don't matter and instead get wrapped up in God. Let's allow God to change our hearts to forgive, let go, and give love a little more. When we live in good measure the good measure will be returned, pressed down, shaken together and running over.

Journal

Day 7

Take time to meditate on God's word. What's on your heart this week?

_____

_____

_____

_____

_____

_____

_____

_____

_____

_____

_____

_____

_____

_____

_____

_____

_____

_____

_____

_____

_____

Week Forty-Seven

Day 1

IN DEED & TRUTH

Lord, You want us to abide in Your love. You want us to not necessarily talk at times and just let Your words seep in. You want us to do good deeds in love, showing the truth in our hearts.

When we see fellow Christians and friends down, we need to help pick them up. We are to serve our brothers and sisters, not giving up on them. We are to support them as You do us.

Lord, help us to love our brothers and sisters as You have loved us. Help us to demonstrate that same love. Keep us grounded in Your love. Let us love others in deed and in truth.

By this we know love, that he laid down his life for us, and we ought to lay down our lives for the brothers. But if anyone has the world's goods and sees his brother in need, yet closes his heart against him, how does God's love abide in him? Little children, let us not love in word or talk but in deed and in truth. 1 John 3:16-18

Lord, let Your love abide in us today, and help us to have open hearts to serve everyone we meet with the same love with which You serve us.

Day 2

FOR THOSE WHO LOVE HIM

We know God loves us, but do we always really believe how vast His love is for us? Do we believe who and what God is through the Holy Spirit that lives inside of us?

We have not received the spirit of the world, but we have received the Spirit of God. That should help us understand the gifts that God has so freely given us.

"What no eye has seen, nor ear heard, nor the heart of man imagined, what God has prepared for those who love him."
1 Corinthians 2:9

That's a pretty bold scripture. No one has ever seen, nor heard, nor can even imagine what God has in store for us. We surely serve a bold God.

We cannot even imagine what He has for us in heaven. It's unfathomable. How amazing is that? We will one day be able to see something we can't even imagine.

He has created a masterpiece for us in heaven, and while we are here, we need to allow Him to create a masterpiece in us.

For those who love Him, He has prepared unimaginable wonders.

Day 3

RUN TO THE WORD

God's word is always right. It should always be the first place we run when we need answers. He gave it to us to show us what to do. All God's work is done in faithfulness. God will never fail us.

As many times that we sin and fall short, God does not and will not leave our sides. In a world so full of tragedy and chaos, we should also be confident in knowing that it is also full of God's unfailing love.

There is always good to be seen. We all need to be an example of God's faithfulness and steadfastness.

Sometimes we need to run. We are overwhelmed and exhausted by our problems, in society and in our own homes. Where do we run? Run to the word. Get into His scripture and read His promises over your life. Run to the principles He has given to guide us.

The word of the Lord will always stand firm.

For the word of the Lord is upright, and all his work is done in faithfulness. Psalm 33:4

Day 4

ULTIMATE PROVIDER

Remember, there are other believers all around you who are going through the same sufferings you are. You are not alone.

God has called you to share in His eternal glory. After you have suffered a little while, he will restore, support, and strengthen you to a place of firm foundation.

The Lord takes away all our anxieties. Our anxieties don't come from the Lord. If you are worried or stressed, then cast it on the Lord. He is the ultimate healer. He is the ultimate provider. Let your faith grow strong.

Without Him we are nothing, but with Him we are everything.

He has overcome the world. Pray, seek and reach out. Through every test there will come a testimony. Don't allow your doubt to outweigh your growth. Stand firm and strong in your faith. Be a witness to others that they aren't in this alone. Humble yourselves before Him so that He may use you as a light to shine, sharing your testimony with others. What you have is a vision of hope for someone else.

Humble yourselves, therefore, under the mighty hand of God so that at the proper time he may exalt you, casting all your anxieties on him, because he cares for you.
1 Peter 5:6-7

Day 5

FOUR POINTS TO SUCCESS

We should strive to have God's love perfected in us. Through my own walk with God, I have found that doing four things helps me to keep the love of God working through me.

"Beloved, if God so loved us, we also ought to love one another. No one has ever seen God; if we love one another, God abides in us and his love is perfected in us."
1 John 4:11-12

1. Believe in His Son
2. Love others as He loves us.
3. Be Faithful
4. Forgive as He has forgiven

Doing these four things can help make all our lives secure in Him. To believe in His Son, Jesus Christ, and what He did for you gives you a place to spend eternity. It gives you a sense of hope, but above all else, it frees you.

Loving one another as He loves us is hard. Sometimes there are unlovable people. God still tells us that if we love one another, then He lives insides of us, and His love can be perfected (completed) in us. When we love even those who are unlovable, God's love is completed through us.

We are to remain faithful to our Father for He remains faithful to us. When someone hurts us, we must not dwell on the hurt. We have to forgive them because we were forgiven. Our debt has been paid, and we have been set free. Who are we to deny forgiveness to someone else?

Day 6

MY REFUGE

When we live for Christ, our actions need to represent that. In our homes we have to learn to keep the peace and not allow the devil to come in to shake it. We must learn to deal with things the way God would have us to.

Even through the tough times we must remember the good in all situations. God has it all handled; why not allow Him to take care of the bad things while allowing us to recognize the good in it all? Our house is our dwelling place.

Do not allow yourself to get consumed with the things you can't control but allow yourself to get consumed in the things God has given you.

The Bible tells us that God is our strength and our refuge. Why not allow that to process when you are struggling? Remember that every time conflict may arise. Allow the presence of God to come into your dwelling place. All it takes is a simple act of prayer asking for Him to come in.

"I will say to the Lord, "My refuge and my fortress, my God, in whom I trust." Psalm 91:2

Day 7

Take time to meditate on God's word. What's on your heart this week?

_____

_____

_____

_____

_____

_____

_____

_____

_____

_____

_____

_____

_____

_____

_____

_____

_____

_____

_____

_____

_____

Week Forty-Eight

Day 1

SIMPLE COMFORT

When Job was attacked by Satan, it seemed that all odds were against him. Everything was taken from him, and he was struck with loathsome sores.

When his three friends heard the news, the Bible says,

They made an appointment together to come to show him sympathy and comfort him. Job 2:11

That brings us to our first point: find friends that will make appointments for you.

For the longest time, I prayed to God seeking friendships. Ones that would help build me, strengthen me, but most importantly, speak the truth to me even when I didn't want to hear it. Those kinds of friends make appointments to build our faith and acknowledge the truth when we are seeking wisdom in trials.

I love the next part of these verses in Job.

And when they saw him from a distance, they did not recognize him. And they raised their voices and wept, and they tore their robes and sprinkled dust of their heads towards the heaven. Job 2:12

When they saw Job and his distress, instead of looking to each other, they looked to the heavens and wept.

Find friends that will weep with you. When someone would tear their clothes, it meant they were in mourning. These friends felt Job's pain and met him in his agony.

And they sat with him on the ground seven days and seven nights, and no one spoke a word to him, for they saw that his suffering was very great. Job 2:13

First, we know Job's friends must have been men because there is no way three women could sit on the ground for seven days and seven nights without at least saying something.

For seven days and seven nights no one spoke, but they sat with him right where he was. I can only imagine in those seven days and seven nights the things someone would want to say, but sometimes simple comfort doesn't come from words. Simple comfort can also come from action. They sat and joined him in is tribulation.

Find friends that will sit with you. Even when the suffering is great, they'll join you on the ground.

Day 2

REPAY EVIL WITH LOVE

Do not repay evil for evil or reviling for reviling, but on the contrary,
bless, for to this you were called, that you may obtain a blessing.
1 Peter 3:9

When someone does something wrong to you, it's so easy to want to do the same in return. What Jesus showed us in the Bible, though, is that even though people treated Him terribly and tried to hurt Him, He still blessed and loved His enemies. God's glory can't be revealed if we repay evil with evil. We must allow God to be the answer and not ourselves. When God moves, He can open the eyes of the other person who is trying to create division. When we allow God to respond, we allow them to see and feel what He needs them to and not what we think they need.

Trust me. It's easy to get caught up in the moment and want to tell someone after they have hurt you just how you feel, but God's response to evil is far better than any response we could ever give. We must trust that when others hurt us God will take care of our feelings. He will help remove the negativity and anger from our hearts.

Lean into Him, so you may obtain your blessing.

Day 3

HE KNOCKS

God is always knocking at our doors. Whether it be for us to rely on Him, to get closer to Him, or to accept Him; He is constantly there knocking. He always wants to be in a relationship with us. One that is everlasting and continues to grow. He is waiting and ready for us to come to have a relationship with Him. One that is deep and loving.

Are you answering the door when he knocks?

Let's invite Him in.

"Behold, I stand at the door and knock. If anyone hears my voice and opens the door, I will come in to him and eat with him, and he with me." Revelations 3:20

If you feel God knocking at your door today, answer it. Let Him come in and be with you. All He desires is a relationship of openness with you. Allow Him some space in you today.

Day 4

IN HIS WHEN

God will answer all our questions, but we have to call to Him and ask Him what we want to know. He will give us the desires of our hearts, but we have to be willing to accept them in His timing.

The closer we get to Him, the more confidence we will have in His word. The more we read His word, the more knowledge we will have stored up when we start to question.

Today, pray for God's timing. His timing is always the best timing. Pray that although you want answers now, your heart grows to know that the answers may come, not in the now, but in His "when." In God's "when" the answers will always be perfect and complete.

He has made everything beautiful in its time.
Ecclesiastes 3:11

Day 5

FIND YOUR STRENGTHS

We all have strengths and weaknesses. Have you ever actually sat down and wrote yours out? I would suggest taking some time and doing it. Seeing what makes you feel really good and what not so much.

I have realized recently that if things don't bring my heart joy based on what the Holy Spirit is speaking into it, then I need to learn to say no. One of my weaknesses has been saying yes too much. Do you have that problem? I would say yes to everyone and everything if I had the chance, and then I'd find myself in a place of regret that I had said yes. The task, the place, or the thing no longer made me happy, and I was feeling remorse for making the decision I did.

This left me in a place of not giving God all of me or the best of me. Instead, I was giving Him what was left over. That's not what God wants for us. When we do things, God wants us to do it all through and in the joy of Him.

We all have our unique strengths and weaknesses, but these are things we should visit more regularly than not. Get in tune with the Holy Spirit and figure out what makes your heart happy. Find your strengths, give God your weaknesses and then let God have the best of you, not the rest of you.

"But seek first the kingdom of God and his righteousness, and all these things will be added to you."
Matthew 6:3

Day 6

Guard Your Heart

Above all else, guard your heart, for everything you do flows from it.
Proverbs 4:23 (NIV)

When we allow things into our hearts, our hearts will begin to show signs of the things we've allowed to take residence in them. Protecting our hearts is very important in our walk with the Lord. When we start to allow others' negative thoughts, words, or actions to have power inside our own hearts, it can begin to contaminate and defile them.

Those who guard their lips preserve their lives,
but those who speak rashly will come to ruin.
Proverbs 13:3 (NIV)

We need to pay close attention to the things we let in, but we also need to pay close attention to the things we let out that could affect someone else's heart.

Our actions come from what's in our hearts. If our hearts are not in a good place, the things we do and say will show it. We must guard what we allow in. This is with all things, not just people. We need to be cautious and know when things or situations may not be of God and to allow discernment to protect our heart. Know when to walk away.

Our hearts are meant to be protected because they're the internal home inside of us for Jesus Christ. Just as we guard our homes and families, we need to make sure we are protecting our hearts.

Journal

Day 7

Take time to meditate on God's word. What's on your heart this week?

_____

_____

_____

_____

_____

_____

_____

_____

_____

_____

_____

_____

_____

_____

_____

_____

_____

_____

Week Forty-Nine

Day 1

GRANTING YOUR DESIRES

I've been thinking a lot lately about prayer, and I have realized that there is something I sometimes fail to do regarding prayer. Maybe you do this, too. Are you specific with your prayers? As specific as we are with those around us when we tell them exactly what we need or want, we are supposed to do the same thing with God.

We are to go to Him and tell Him exactly what we need and want. Sometimes my prayers can be simple, and there is nothing wrong with simple prayers, but we don't serve a simple God. I want my prayers to be powerful, huge, expectant prayers. Asking God for exactly what I want to happen in my marriage, in my children, at my job, or even with my dreams. I want to specifically bring Him the desires of my heart and believe that what He can do with those desires are more than I could ever imagine or dream.

God knows our hearts' desires, but He also wants to hear them.

"And I tell you, ask, and it will be given to you; seek, and you will find; knock, and it will be opened to you."
Luke 11:9

Ask, and it will be given to you. What are you not specifically asking God for? God wants to grant all your desires.

Day 2

QUITTING IS NOT AN OPTION

What if all the well-known men and women of the Bible had decided to quit? What if Joseph didn't live out his dreams? What if Peter gave up on fishing? Say Mary ran from baring Jesus, or Naomi kept drowning in her own sorrow. If they would have quit, we wouldn't have the stories we have now that lead us to His faithfulness.

Quitting is not an option when it comes to living the life God calls us to live. Just as in these stories we see how His faithfulness prevails in our own testimonies and walks.

I have wanted quitting to be my option many times when it has come to life. It seemed things would be a lot easier if I could just walk away or be done. There have actually been many times I chose to walk away and just be done. Getting pregnant at seventeen was a situation that came with many struggles and obstacles. Lord knows I wanted to throw in the towel many times when parenting or even being a wife. It's funny, though, because from our homes to our jobs and decisions we make every day, we have the option to quit, but we also have the option to start.

Start one more day. Start one more hour. Start one more minute succumbing to His will and purpose over our lives. I challenge you today to think about the start instead of the quit!

And let us not grow weary of doing good, for in due season we will reap, if we do not give up.
Galatians 6:9

Day 3

ORGANIZE YOUR THOUGHTS

I don't know about you, but my thoughts sometimes run rapid. I'll be thinking of all the things I have to get done, and I truly forget the purpose behind even doing them.

Please tell me I'm not alone in needing to organize my thoughts like I organize my closet. I can keep like-colored clothes together and my shoes neat and tidy, but sometimes my thoughts just get the best of me.

I have learned from Jesus' walk while here on earth that sometimes it's best to step away. Jesus would take time to go and pray, and in a lot of those instances, He would go alone.

When our thoughts seem disorganized or too much, maybe that's the time to recognize we ourselves need a time-out to pray, a step away to organize our thoughts. If the Savior of the world needed a time-out, I'm pretty sure I may need to put myself in one every so often as well.

Gathering anything takes time. It takes dedication and willingness. Gather your thoughts today. Organize them, declutter them, and take a time-out if needed.

Complete my joy by being of the same mind, having the same love,
being in full accord and of one mind.
Philippians 2:2

Day 4

WHAT, YOU NEED MORE?

When Jesus fed 5000 off five loaves of bread and two fish, I can only imagine Him thinking, "What, you need more?" It's never about what we have, but what He can do with what we have. These men didn't see a lot in what they had, but Jesus looked up to heaven and said a blessing.

And he said to them, "How many loaves do you have? Go and see." And when they had found out, they said, "Five, and two fish." Then he commanded them all to sit down in groups on the green grass. So they sat down in groups, by hundreds and by fifties. And taking the five loaves and the two fish, he looked up to heaven and said a blessing and broke the loaves and gave them to the disciples to set before the people. And he divided the two fish among them all. And they all ate and were satisfied. And they took up twelve baskets full of broken pieces and of the fish. And those who ate the loaves were five thousand men. Mark 6:38-44

There is something about looking up to heaven for the blessing. These men weren't lacking just a little, they were lacking a lot.

Is there something you need more of today? Don't look down on the problem; look up to the blessing. Take in His word and be satisfied.

Day 5

OWN THE CHANGE

Have you ever felt like you were in a period of transition? Maybe a period of waiting. You may feel like God has you in the processing stage, and you're not sure what the change is going to look like.

Don't we all go through periods of change, periods when we are processing through things waiting for our answers from God? I have realized that after my periods of transition comes bigger transformation. Everything that has to go through a process ends with change.

God is constantly having to reshape us into who He is calling us to be.

Own the change God has created for you. I can't imagine owning change, but I think that may be the place God wants us to be in - a place where we no longer tense up at the sight of it, but we allow God to change us from the inside out, over and over again.

And we all, who with unveiled faces contemplate the Lord's glory, are being transformed into his image with ever-increasing glory, which comes from the Lord, who is the spirit. 2 Corinthians 3:18 (NIV)

Day 6

CAN'T HIDE FOR LONG

As I sat here with the cursor going back and forth pondering my thoughts, I received a text from a friend who was struggling, wanting to hide and wanting to run in the opposite direction of where she knew she was being called. Goodness, isn't that the reality of what we all do at times? We would like to find a hiding place and not come out for a little bit.

We can't hide for long, though. You see, Jesus showed us that when he was questioned in the book of John. The Jews thought Jesus had a demon inside of him. They couldn't quite understand how Jesus could be greater than Abraham, but how Jesus answers them and what He does is something we can all learn from.

Jesus answered, "If I glorify myself, my glory is nothing. It is my Father who glorifies me, of whom you say, 'He is our God.' But you have not known him. I know him. If I were to say that I do not know him, I would be a liar like you, but I do know him and I keep his word. Your father Abraham rejoiced that he would see my day. He saw it and was glad." So the Jews said to him, "You are not yet fifty years old, and have you seen Abraham?" Jesus said to them, "Truly, truly, I say to you, before Abraham was, I am." So they picked up stones to throw at him, but Jesus hid himself and went out of the temple. John 8:54-59

What stones are being thrown at you causing you to want to hide? You see, before Jesus hid Himself, he proclaimed the word of God, but something I love even more is that Jesus threw these men a little shade. "If I were to say that I do not know him, I would be a liar like you, but I do know

him, and I keep his word." I would be a liar like you. Well there, Jesus, I'd be a liar if I didn't say I like your honesty.

Jesus knew from where His glory came, and He also knew who "I am" was, but He had to protect Himself. He knew how important it is was to go into hiding to keep His word. Fight the enemy with his own tactics. You aren't a liar, you are a child in the word. The problem here is not actually us trying to hide but having discernment of when it's time to hide. Jesus knew he needed to hide and go out of the temple. His discernment was in the will of God.

Is there something you need to call the enemy out on? Pray that you have the discernment to go into hiding when the enemy starts to throw stones. However, make sure that you run into hiding in the direction of God and not away from Him.

Journal

Day 7

Take time to meditate on God's word. What's on your heart this week?

_____

_____

_____

_____

_____

_____

_____

_____

_____

_____

_____

_____

_____

_____

_____

_____

_____

_____

_____

Week Fifty

Day 1

CONFUSION AT ITS FINEST

Doesn't the enemy love to come all up in our business and confuse the mess out of us at times, making us question all we know that's right?

Even the people that seem as if they have it all together fight with sin. Confusion is a weapon the enemy uses against us. He will mix up or disorient our thoughts so that we can't clearly see the facts laid out in front of us.

Leave your impoverished confusion and live!
Proverbs 9:6 (MSG)

Any thoughts that aren't well thought out can cause confusion. We need to leave our confusion for the certainty God has given us through His word and live!

Day 2

SPIRIT OF GENTLENESS

I don't know about you, but when I was reading about the spirit of gentleness, I felt like I have a thing or two I could learn. Being gentle with others is something we should do all the time and in any circumstance.

Brothers, if anyone is caught in any transgressions, you who are spiritual should restore him in a spirit of gentleness. Keep watch on yourself, lest you too be tempted. Bear one another's burdens, and fulfill the law of Christ.
Galatians 6:1-2

We should restore in a spirit of gentleness. This means those around us that are caught in any transgressions (offense, wrong-doings, misbehavior, sin), we are to help rebuild them with gentleness. Gentleness is how Jesus served others time and time again throughout scripture.

When we respond in gentleness, we are rebuilding and restoring others through Christ-like behavior, being gentle in our response and in our actions.

If you've ever gone to help another sister or brother in sin, you know that you yourself can be tempted in actions or in speech. This is why it warns us that first we must respond in gentleness, but we need to be careful to not become tempted as well. If we aren't responding in gentleness, we can get caught up in starting to judge or condemn them when we have been called to love. We are to help carry their burdens, lightening their load so that Christ's love can be shown through us in our actions and speech. This is such a powerful scripture that teaches us the importance of

being gentle with those around us. When we are gentle, kind, and tenderhearted to others, we are able to build them up while allowing God to use us, but when we are unsympathetic or hardhearted, we can begin to tear down what God is trying to restore.

Who can you offer a gentle spirit to today?

Day 3

SUPPORT GROUP

Did you know that Jesus had an inner circle? In His inner circle there were those who were closest to Him, those to whom He would go, His support group. Jesus had twelve disciples, but He had three in the twelve who were His closest people.

Do you have a support group, others that you may say are your people? Everyone needs support from those around them, but we all also need an inner circle. Those we are closest to in whom we can confide, share our lives with, and count on when the going gets tough.

Jesus' inner circle consisted of Peter, James, and John. Your inner circle may consist of less or more. The number in the inner circle doesn't matter as much as the heart of the inner circle. The heart of the inner circle should be that they are for you. They stand in the gap when it needs to be filled. They tell the truth when truth needs to be told, and they not only have your best interest inside their own hearts, but they feel your heart, embrace your pain, and lighten your load.

If you are blessed with an inner circle, even if it's one person, thank them today.

A man of many companions may come to ruin, but there is a friend
who sticks closer than a brother.
Proverbs 18:24

Day 4

OUR MINISTRY IS EACH OTHER

In Acts we see Peter using an opportunity to pour out to those who are lost. That's our ministry here. Are we pouring out our love and adoration for God while sharing the gospel in the hopes of teaching those who are lost?

Peter poured out the word of God with authority. He brought others to Christ even though he would be persecuted for doing so. He frustrated some, but he saved many.

But many of those who had heard the word believed, and the number of the men came about five thousand.
Acts 4:4

Sometimes the only thing that someone may need is to hear the word. Think about being in one of your most desperate places with the word of God to help you through, and then think about yourself in the same situation without it. What a huge difference knowing God's promises can make in a desperate situation.

You don't just have to preach to share the word. Sharing the word can come through the discipline in your life. God's word can reflect in your own obedience and walk. Your testimony can be the goodness someone needs to hear.

Share what you know and let others in on the good news that He brings today. Let our ministry be each other.

Day 5

INTERCEDES ON OUR BEHALF

And he who searches hearts knows what is the mind of the Spirit, because the Spirit intercedes for the saints according to the will of God. Romans 8:27

Hearing this scripture gives me a look into a promise for us all. Do you know what the word intercede means? It means to intervene on someone's behalf. To step in. God does this with us, His children. He intercedes with His Spirit and intervenes in situations and circumstances on our behalf.

He is our advocate or our spokesperson at times when we feel we can't speak at all.

There have been times I have been deep in prayer and have lost all words. Nothing else would come to mind, but I also had an overwhelming feeling that I knew it was okay to not have any words. Even though I drew a blank, I didn't feel blank. That was the intercession of the Spirit.

God searches our hearts and minds and knows what's inside of them. So when the words don't seem to form, or there is nothing that we can say, the Spirit can intercede as a spokesperson for us.

Have you ever not been able to form the words to pray? God knows your mind and your heart. He searches it and will intercede according to His will.

Day 6

MISSED THE MARK

A lot of us have been told we can't have negative feelings. You know the ones when we are sad, angry, anxious, or maybe worried. I know I have been told before that they are all from the enemy, and I need to get rid of those feelings immediately; that God doesn't want us to feel like that. I agree that He doesn't want us to feel like that because He ultimately wants us happy, but I do think God wants us to feel our feelings. They give us passion with our purpose.

As I drove down the road the other day, I thought to myself that we may be missing the mark. What if what we sometimes may be telling others isn't exactly true? I think our feelings all have a reason, and we should embrace them. The thing is we have to be careful what we do with them.

Jesus was perfect, but He still had feelings while He was here. You see, He wept. He got angry and flipped a table. We even know that He could have been anxious or worried right before His crucifixion when He went to God about what was about to happen.

He withdrew about a stone's throw beyond them, knelt down and prayed, "Father, if you are willing, take this cup from me; yet not my will, but yours be done."
Luke 22:41-42 (NIV)

Jesus was sinless, but He wasn't emotionless.

You may think when you feel sad, angry, or depressed that it's just the enemy, or you can't talk to anyone about it

because you aren't supposed to feel that way and be a Christian. I'm here to tell you that nothing could be further from the truth.

Feel your feelings, just don't escape in them or allow them to cause you to sin. Grab onto God in those feelings just as you see Jesus did. Grab a friend. Make sure you have an accountability partner to come alongside you and help. Just know you aren't in it alone. Jesus even felt, but He knelt.

Today we know that if we are living, we are feeling. Take those feelings and kneel down to Him in prayer. If you are feeling so is God.

Journal

Day 7

Take time to meditate on God's word. What's on your heart this week?

_____

_____

_____

_____

_____

_____

_____

_____

_____

_____

_____

_____

_____

_____

_____

_____

_____

_____

_____

Week Fifty-One

Day 1

BEING IN TUNE

One day I decided to sing a song with my daughter, thinking we could do a duet. She has a beautiful voice and so do I (in the shower and car), but when I removed the music from behind our voices, I sounded like nails on a chalkboard. I wasn't in tune for anything and very fast had to give up the dream of ever becoming a famous vocalist.

Have you ever felt out of tune in your relationship with God? I know I have, but when you feel in tune, it's one of the best feelings there could be.

When I talk about being in tune with God, I mean when you value His guidance in your decisions and everyday life, and you can almost hear Him speaking to your heart.

Jesus was in tune with His Father. We may not be able to be as in tune as They were, but we do have the Holy Spirit living inside of us. Jesus walked in confidence. He knew God's plan while He was here, and He stepped in purpose. We too should want to be in tune with God. I want to walk in the confidence of making the right decisions, seeking Him out before I decide. I want to value His opinion so much that before I go to anyone else, I always go to Him.

I don't know about you, but I want to be so in tune that I don't need the background music (all the other people or things). Those are bonuses He sends me, but my relationship with Him is built on our voices together.

Draw near to God, and he will draw near to you.
James 4:8

Day 2

THE STRUGGLE IS REAL

Isn't this the truth!

What's your struggle? We all have them; Jesus even had struggles. He dealt with loneliness, grief, pain, and rejection.

You see, we aren't exempt from the struggle, but what we do during it matters is what matters. Are you currently struggling with something? I have shared that one of my struggles is self-doubt. I doubt my abilities as a mom, a wife, a friend, a speaker, and a writer. I doubt the talents God has given me and fear not doing them to the best of my ability. The problem with doubt is that God has and always will give us more than enough.

If you need help with your struggle, don't feel ashamed, and get the help you need. Sometimes it takes more than you to fix the struggle and that's okay. Go to God first, and then call a counselor or speak to your pastor.

Don't let your struggle grip you. You have the option to grip back!

And my God will supply every need of yours according to his riches in glory in Christ Jesus.
Philippians 4:19

Day 3

HEART CRIES

Sometimes worship comes from such a deep place that your heart cries.

There is an intimate place of worship that comes in the sincerity of our most desperate pleas. The pleas where our tender hearts truly know nothing other than, "Lord, I'm struggling to put the pieces together. I'm struggling to know the words to praise, but I know you are sovereign. I know you are a good Father, and in the midst of my troubled heart, I will worship you in my admiration for you."

This is a place of worship that is unexplainable, untouchable, and indescribable. It's a place where surrender begins to happen, and your eyes well with what your heart so desperately knows. He is holding you. There are no distractions and there is nothing happening other than His love being poured out over you.

Those are heart cries. When there are no words to form and more tears than it seems one eye could possibly contain. Those tears come from a place that only He is able to abide in. I felt God today deep in my heart cry.

It was not just me weeping, for
"Jesus wept."
John 11:35

They're not just your tears they're His too. Worship when your heart cries!

Day 4

SELFLESS INTENTION

We consume ourselves with too much sometimes. You know that saying, "Stop and smell the roses"? How often do we actually stop and breathe in the air He has created for us - the actual deep intake of His Holy Spirit filling our lungs?

We get so immersed in the hustle and bustle of life that we begin to not see those sweet God-filled moments that can present themselves all around us. I'll be the first to admit, I have been too caught up in my busyness, my expectations, or my wants that I have previously failed to see His desires over my day. Anyone else?

We shouldn't want to miss out on these opportunities.

This is the life you breathe out onto others. Are we loving them, portraying Christ, and taking time out of our days to remember their needs as well? We should work on letting go of selfish ambition and digging into selfless intention.

Allow your intake and outtake today to be Holy Spirit led and fed, selflessly being intentional with each breath your breathe.

"The Spirit of God has made me, and the breath of the Almighty gives me life." Job 33:4

Day 5

FIGHT THROUGH THE PAIN

I've never physically been in a boxing ring, but at times I've felt there mentally. The punches that a boxer takes in a ring somehow start to compare to the real life punches we take in life. One by one, those punches can start to become more painful, and just as a boxer you find yourself fighting through them.

A boxer can take many physical punches and somehow mentally keep themselves together in the ring, fighting through the pain. We take many mental punches in life and have to continue to fight through the pain.

The difference between the two is what's leading the way. What is leading you through the pain?

When training, boxers don't just train for endurance and physical well-being, they mentally prepare themselves for the fight. We may sometimes get blindsided by our battles, but we have to be prepared to fight.

Are you prepared for battle?

It's not promised that we won't have fights in our lives. That's why we must be prepared.

Read up, kneel down in prayer, and keep your feet planted firmly on the ground.

A boxer knows that a perfect stance in the ring gives him power and mobility and is crucial to his fight. We know that our feet planted on God is crucial for the stability we

need in our fight. What stance do you have; what's the position of your feet?

He makes me as surefooted as a deer, enabling me to stand on mountain heights. Psalm 18:33 (NLT)

Day 6

WHEN HE SAYS REST

I don't know about you, but when stress hits me, I feel like I need a supernatural intervention. Recently through the difficult time we have had to face with my grandmother's cancer diagnosis, I have realized that I don't need an intervention, I just need sweet rest with my Father.

You see, every day our brain takes in so many things. It takes in the reality of life and other things that we may not have planned. On top of just everyday things, we are also taking in other people's lives through social media. Our brains are overwhelmed with life because we feed it so many details, but our hearts are just yearning for rest.

For a long time, I thought rest was just lying down, taking a nap, reading a book, or just journaling to God. Rest is so much more. God is needing us to be still, but to be still in Him. Rest for our bodies sometimes takes 8 hours. We need rest to rejuvenate ourselves for the next day and to be prepared to face the world, but we also need mental rest in the word. Sometimes that means taking out everything that you normally do and replacing it with just Him. I love podcasts, worship music, and I even just picked up the love for reading. God loves us feeding ourselves with those things too. We are learning and engaging in things that He also loves. They aren't bad things we are digesting, but God sometimes just needs us to be fed with Him.

You know how Jesus would go to those desolate places just to be with God? We may not be able to do that literally, but we can cut off all noise and rest. Even the good noise.

Take a day, two days, maybe even a week and just take in only the noise of you and Him, resting your brain and your heart from everything except Him.

Let Him make all the noise feeding into you. Whether it be in sweet silence or through seeing and hearing His creation all around you. Open the word and let Him be the only one to speak.

Take time to truly rest.

"Come to me, all who labor and are heavy laden, and I will give you rest." Matthew 11:28

Journal

Day 7

Take time to meditate on God's word. What's on your heart this week?

_____

_____

_____

_____

_____

_____

_____

_____

_____

_____

_____

_____

_____

_____

_____

_____

_____

_____

_____

Week Fifty-Two

Day 1

LAUNCHING PAD

Have you ever been working on something, whether it be on yourself or something else, and just felt like you took a few steps back? I used to see those steps back as bad; they were almost something to frown upon. What if we shifted that perspective?

What if those steps back were launching us forward? This may be your take off!

Think about it. When a quarterback goes to throw the ball, he pulls his arm back to get the momentum and power he needs to get the ball across the field. When an arrow goes in a bow to be shot, you have to pull it back before you can aim it and let it go.

What if those steps back are what is giving you the momentum to take the next few steps forward?

That energy is God's energy, an energy deep within you, God himself willing and working at what will give him the most pleasure.
Philippians 2:13 (MSG)

It's not about our pleasure; each step is to give God the glory. The next time you feel like you have taken a few steps back, use whatever place you are in as your launching pad.

Day 2

SIT AT HIS FEET

As I read through the Bible, I realize sin was just as prevalent then as it is now. Bad things happened, and good people would fall down. Jesus walked the earth then and continues to walk it through us. I realize a lot is the same, but one thing that is different is the amount of distractions keeping us away from being in deep connection with others and loving well.

Now as they went on their way, Jesus entered a village. And a woman named Martha welcomed him into her house. And she had a sister called Mary, who sat at the Lord's feet and listened to his teaching. But Martha was distracted with much serving. And she went up to him and said, "Lord, do you not care that my sister has left me to serve alone? Tell her then to help me." But the Lord answered her, "Martha, Martha, you are anxious and troubled about many things, but one thing is necessary. Mary has chosen the good portion, which will not be taken away from her."
Luke 10:38-42

You see, Martha welcomed Jesus into her house a lot like you and I welcome Him into our lives. We want to receive Him; we want to be in a relationship with Him. She even had good intentions of wanting to serve Him, but she missed the point. Goodness, don't we all miss the point sometimes? She was so preoccupied by serving that she wasn't able to love Him well.

I don't know about you, but I don't want to be so wrapped up in all the distractions that this world can offer that I forget to love well and be intentional in my relationship with

Christ.   It's so easy to get so preoccupied by everything around us that we start missing the point. You see, Martha was so wrapped up in the distractions that she began to point the finger at Mary for not helping her. Could you be pointing a finger because your heart is overwhelmed, anxious, and troubled?

Mary dropped it all to sit as His feet. We have a lot to learn from Mary in this story. We need to remember to drop it all and sit as His feet. I don't know about you, but I want to love Him well!

Day 3

WHAT'S YOUR POSITION?

One thing I know is that no matter your walk, there will always be naysayers. Before the Passover Jesus went to have dinner with Lazarus, Mary, and Martha. As Martha served and Lazarus reclined at the table with Jesus, Mary took the time to love on Him in another way. As Mary showed her love for Jesus, Judas thought what Mary was doing was a waste.

Mary therefore took a pound of expensive ointment made from pure nard, and anointed the feet of Jesus and wiped his feet with her hair. The house was filled with the fragrance of the perfume. But Judas Iscariot, one of his disciples (he who was about the betray him), said, "Why was this ointment not sold for three hundred denarii and given to the poor?"' John 12:3-5

You see, the heart of Judas was in the wrong place, but Mary came before Jesus in humility. Isn't it truly all about the position of our hearts? Judas was a naysayer and was thinking about how this affected him. Mary, on the other hand, wasn't thinking of herself at all, and instead she was thinking of how she could serve Him.

Nothing is ever a waste laid at the feet of Jesus. There will always be something or someone telling you otherwise, but what you do for Him shows the position of your heart.

Let's position our hearts in humility for Him every day, and God will work out the rest with those around us. Let's not be a Judas serving Jesus for what we can gain, but let's be a Mary serving Jesus with all we can give.

Day 4

UNWRAP YOUR GIFTS

Quick question, are you making the most out of what you've been given?

This is actually a question I read in a book I decided to re-read after our pastor preached on fresh vision one Sunday. This is a question I feel like we should be asking ourselves regularly.

Everything we have is a gift from God. As I reflect on the last few days opening gifts or seeing others unwrapping their gifts, I can't help but think about their excitement or the anticipation I felt leading up to their reactions.

Can you imagine that we have a God that is always doing the same? He is always excited for us. He gives us gifts regularly. Sometimes what we've been given we even decided to unwrap and lay to the side. He has the anticipation and excitement for us, and instead, we choose to be envious of other people's gifts or just not appreciate the fullness of the gifts He gives us.

Everything we unwrap here is a gift from God. What are you doing with those gifts after you receive them? I would suggest today that you sit down and write a list of the precious gifts God has given you and see if you are making the most out of them. I will be joining you.

God gives unique gifts to each of us. What He has for you isn't going to be the same as He has for me. God wants us to make the best of who we are, and He gives us gifts based

on those abilities. We were all created uniquely inside of His image.

We are going into this New Year, no matter the circumstance, with many God-given gifts. The gifts of redemption, grace, love, peace, comfort, and trust. We get to enter into those gifts in this new year with new perspective. How will you use your gifts?

Let's make the most of what we've been given this year!

Everything comes from him; Everything happens through him; Everything ends up in him. Always glory! Always Praise! Yes. Yes. Yes. Romans 11:36 (MSG)

Day 5

JUST A LITTLE MORE

It's not always about taking leaps and bounds. Sometimes it's just about taking a step in the right direction.

I was talking to a good friend once and realized that sometimes we get so caught up in wanting to see progress that we want change to take place rapidly, and we forget good things take time. You see, with answers at the click of a mouse and even with a quick saying of a name, "Alexa," we tend to forget that some answers from God just take time.

Jesus was reported by most scholars to be alive for about 33 years. If it took Jesus 33 years to teach, heal, save, and raise people, including himself, from the dead, don't you think that it's going to take us, as sinners, some time to get it right? Life isn't a race. It's a step by step process, each day deciding to put one foot in front of the other, taking the right steps in the direction of Christ.

Decide to trust just a little more. Love just a little more. Pray just a little more. Read just a little more. Be kind just a little more. Share Jesus just a little more. Sacrifice just a little more. Forgive just a little more. Just a little more. One more step leading closer to Him is better than no step at all. Decide today to take just one more step.

Steady my steps with your Word of promise so nothing malign gets the better of me. Psalm 119:133 (MSG)

Day 6

COME EXPECTANT

Moses' unexpectant heart reminds me so much of the way I have been at times. You see, God shows himself to Moses time and time again. Once through his staff by turning it into a snake. Once with him raising his staff and parting the Red Sea. Now Moses finds himself in another predicament. The people God has told him to bring out of Egypt are thirsty with nothing to drink.

So Moses cried to the Lord, "What shall I do with this people? They are almost ready to stone me."
Exodus 17:4

Much like us when we have nowhere else to run, or we are all out of our own efforts we cry out to the Lord, "What do I do, God?" Sometimes we forget that God is our Rock. We forget that Has provided before, and we are no longer expectant of what we know He can do.

And the Lord said to Moses, "Pass on before the people, taking with you some of the elders of Israel, and take in your hand the staff with which you struck the Nile, and go. Behold, I will stand before you there on the rock at Horeb, and you shall strike the rock, and water shall come out of it, and the people will drink."
Exodus 17:5-6

You see, Moses had the staff in his hand all along. It was his support and his weapon. He had used it before. He also had his cry. We all have the right tools, we just fail to use them at times. God has given us what we need to get through the obstacles that may come our way. We have our

weapon and our support in the word. We have our cry through our pleas and our prayers.

God will lead us to Him, The Rock, all we have to do is come to Him expectant of what we know He can do. I am a witness from many times in my past that He always will make the waters flow.

Journal

Day 7

Take time to meditate on God's word. What's on your heart this week?

_____

_____

_____

_____

_____

_____

_____

_____

_____

_____

_____

_____

_____

_____

_____

_____

_____

_____

_____

_____

_____

TAKE SOME TIME

If you started reading this devotional at the beginning of the year, you will end with one extra day before you start your next year. I always love to use the end of the year as a reflection period. I personally love to go back on my year and take the time to thank Him for all the many ways He has poured His love over myself and my family.

Take today and reflect on this last year. Write down the good and the bad. Spend some time thinking of the things you'd like to do again and the things you wished you would have said no to. Take time to rejoice through all the seasons the year brought and praise Him.

Today is such a special day. You've gone through another year. You've pushed yourself a little bit more, and you've accomplished spending quiet time with your Lord. Whether it was every day, or you skipped a few, you are creating lasting memories with Him and building your faith on the One who doesn't falter.

Remember to pat yourself on the back. Love yourself and others much deeper and continue to be all He has created you to be.

My prayer for you

Dear Heavenly Father, thank you for this special
soul. Thank you for creating them uniquely in Your
image. Lord, I pray they continue to create lasting
memories building an intimate relationship with You as
their Father. I pray that as they go into this next year, they
step in it with confidence. Lord, I pray that You just help
them to remember that their worth in this world is far more
than any temporary fleshly feelings. Thank You for blessing
me with the opportunity to use my words to pour into them
through these pages. Lord, use us for Your glory. We love
You.

Amen

Notes:

1. **Week 20, Day 3**
    Graham, Billy, et al. Billy Graham in Quotes. Thomas
    Nelson, 2011.

2. **Week 22, Day 3**
    "The Definition of Peace." Www.dictionary.com,
    www.dictionary.com/browse/peace?s=t.

3. **Week 26, Day 1**
    Bible action songs: Featuring songs from Hes got the whole
    world in His hands, Jesus loves me this I know & This little
    light of mine [CD]. (1998). Everland Entertainment.

4. **Week 28, Day 6**
    Warren, Rick. The Purpose Driven Life: What on Earth Am
    I Here For? Zondervan, 2009.

5. **Week 31, Day 4**
    "The Definition of Freedom." www.dictionary.com,
    www.dictionary.com/browse/freedom

6. **Week 36, Day 6**
    Graham, Billy, et al. Billy Graham in Quotes. Thomas
    Nelson, 2011.

7. **Week 40, Day 4**
    Definition of SELF-PITY. (n.d.). Retrieved from
    https://www.merriam-webster.com/dictionary/self-pity

Let's Connect:

I would love to hear from you on how God is working in your life. Also, if you would like to be added to the daily devotion email list you can email me at the address below. Thank you for sharing your year with me!

Feel free to connect with me through these two ways,

Email:
Faithfullyfaithful7@yahoo.com

Or

Women's Ministry:
www.facebook.com/three.four.one